*The Art of Film Music*

*Music advisor to Northeastern University Press*
GUNTHER SCHULLER

# THE ART *of* FILM MUSIC

George Burt

*Special emphasis on*

Hugo Friedhofer
Alex North
David Raksin
Leonard Rosenman

*Northeastern University Press*
BOSTON

Northeastern University Press

*Library of Congress Cataloging-in-Publication Data*

Burt, George.
    The art of film music : special emphasis on Hugo Friedhofer, Alex
North, David Raksin, Leonard Rosenman / George Burt.
        p.   cm.
    Includes bibliographical references (p.   ) and index.
    ISBN 1-55553-193-8 (cloth: alk. paper)—ISBN 1-55553-270-5
(pbk.: alk. paper)
    1. Motion picture music—Instruction and study. 2. Motion picture mu-
sic—Analysis, appreciation. I. Title.
MT64.M65B87    1994
781.5'42—dc20                94-6521

Designed by Diane Levy

Composed in Bembo by Graphic Composition, Inc., Athens, Georgia.
Printed and bound by Maple Press, York, Pennsylvania. The paper is
Sebago Antique, an acid-free stock.

MANUFACTURED IN THE UNITED STATES OF AMERICA
98   97              5   4   3

# Contents

# Introductory Remarks

A short while ago, Steven Kovacs, chairman of the Film Department at San Francisco State University, invited me to give a series of lectures on film music, knowing that I had been working on a book that was intended for both composers and filmmakers. He said that while his students lacked formal training in music, he felt nevertheless that it was very important for them to have a basic understanding of how music worked in film.

I couldn't have agreed more with this sentiment. It is obvious that music plays a vital role in film, and filmmakers need to have as clear an idea as possible about what they can reasonably ask of the music. Many teachers from various parts of the country have expressed the same view. They point out that there are only a few books on the subject, and these are either on the history of film music, which is interesting and informative, or they are written for a trained musician, which is hard for them to understand. One person said, "I've read these books, or tried to, but I still don't have a feeling for what to say to a composer. I mean, I don't have a picture of what's involved or how to go about it."

Looking at the situation from another point of view, I have heard similar concerns from composers, even fully trained concert composers. Many have confessed that they would give their right arm to score a feature-length film, but even if they had the opportunity, they would have to take some kind of crash course before tackling a film score.

I honestly don't know of anything that would fully prepare a composer to score a film, but I do know that by looking at what established composers have done in specific situations, it is possible to get a feeling for what is involved. The actual mechanics of film scoring can be learned relatively fast, although there always seems to be something else to find out about.

viii    Introductory Remarks

What is not so easily learned is the cinematic language as it relates to music. All of us have grown up with the movies, and to one degree or another, all of us have been moved by certain films. We feel that we are at home with the medium. And to a large extent most of us are. But it is quite another thing to view a film print before music has been added and arrive at deep-seated convictions about where music is needed and the kind of music that would be most helpful to the film.

In this medium, it is absolutely necessary for composers and directors to communicate with each other. Yet communication between them is generally difficult. Even the most creative and highly skilled professionals on both sides regularly complain of this problem.

Why is this? Music is an intricate and specialized language, and talking about musical matters is exceedingly problematic for non-musicians. Musical terminology alone is a barrier. Further, there often is a confusion about what music can and cannot do, a confusion about the difference between literary and musical values. And there is an erroneous but widespread assumption that certain kinds of music are inevitably required in certain situations. For instance, many believe that if people are running, the music should also "run." This is a limiting if not disturbing concept.

These are just a few of the most problematic areas in film music. There are, of course, many others. What this book does is explore these areas as they occur within broad contexts: characterization, accent, pacing, and so on. No prior technical knowledge of either film or music is assumed. The music analyses vary in depth, and most will prove to be relatively clear to non-musicians. A glossary of basic musical terms is included at the back of the book. However, some aspects of the analyses will not be clear to non-musicians because advanced music-analytical terminology is employed. Technical commentary has been placed in italics and may be skipped by non-musicians without loss of continuity.

The book cites many films. In fact, only on rare occasions is an issue explored without reference to a specific film segment. In my judgment, the validity of a statement about artistic matters depends to a large extent on the choice of example within a given analytical context. When confronted with a question about film music, experienced film composers invariably say: "It depends on the situation."

It will be noted that a great deal of space is devoted to a description of the dramatic situations involved. This is necessary in light of the premise of the book: In filmmaking, the drama is the primary concern; music performs a complementary role. Thus, continual reference to plot is indispensable to any discussion of how music functions in film.

Most of the films in the book are from the 1940s through the 1970s;

several are taken from the 1930s and the 1980s. Most if not all the examples are generally regarded as "classic" films, which are screened regularly (especially on television) and are easily available at video stores. I have made this choice principally because the shelf life of new or rarely shown films is impossible to predict, and many disappear after only a short time. Thus, further study of them would be difficult. It is possible that a few readers may find it a bother to acquaint themselves with "older" movies. I would urge them to do so; it will be worth the trouble. These are, after all, great films.

I regret that actual musical scores of Korngold, Steiner, Waxman, and Newman are not included in the book. And there are some thirty or forty other composers also not included who have made significant contributions to the film music world—particularly Rozsa, Tiomkin, Webb, and Kaper from the early period; Copland and Herrmann from the middle period; certainly Goldsmith, Williams, and Morricone of today and, recently, Bruce Broughton and James Horner, to mention but a few. Inclusion of these composers alone would go a long way toward satisfying any expectation as regards historical perspective. However, this is not a book on the history of film music. I feel strongly that although styles change, the challenges discussed in the book emerge out of the medium itself, not as they would in one decade or another or, certainly, with any particular composer.

In short, unique structural, dramaturgical, and perceptual possibilities readily emerge when music is combined with film. In this study, an effort has been made to uncover and examine many of these possibilities so as to arrive at a better understanding of how, when, and on what basis the two media interrelate.

Finally, it would be impossible for me to find the words to express my depth of gratitude to David Raksin, Alex North, and Leonard Rosenman. This book never could have been written without their help and friendship over many years. Thanks are also due to John Addison and Ernest Gold for their generous and invaluable contributions and to Hugo Friedhofer's daughter, Karyl Gilland-Tonge, for making her father's manuscripts available to me. I am indebted to Professor Arthur Gottschalk for his work on the manuscript in its early stages, and to Gunther Schuller for his help and support in bringing this manuscript to publication; to my colleagues, Professors Richard Lavenda and Ellsworth Milburn, Sam Jones, and Paul Cooper for their sustained help and encouragement; and to Tse-Ying Koh and Sally Baker-Carr for their invaluable editorial assistance. Of course, my deepest heartfelt gratitude goes to Sharon and my two sons, Eric and Wylie, for their patience, love, and understanding.

*Acknowledgments*

I wish to thank the following for their willingness to allow me to reproduce excerpts from the scores for the films listed below.

*Al Capone.* Music by David Raksin. Used by permission of David Raksin.

*The Best Years of Our Lives.* Music by Hugo Friedhofer. Copyright 1946 by Samuel Goldwyn. All rights reserved.

*Between Heaven and Hell.* Music by Hugo Friedhofer. Copyright 1956, c/o EMI Robbins Catalog Inc. Reprinted by permission of CPP/Belwin, Inc., Miami, Fla. All rights reserved.

*A Bridge Too Far.* Music by John Addison. Copyright 1977 by United Artists, c/o EMI U Catalog Inc. Reprinted by permission of CPP/Belwin, Inc., Miami, Fla. All rights reserved.

*The Children's Hour.* Music by Alex North. Copyright 1962, c/o EMI U Catalog Inc. Reprinted by permission of CPP/Belwin, Inc., Miami, Fla. All rights reserved.

*Death of a Salesman.* Music by Alex North. Copyright 1983, c/o EMI Mills Catalog Inc. Reprinted by permission of CPP/Belwin, Inc., Miami, Fla. All rights reserved.

*East of Eden.* Music by Leonard Rosenman. Copyright 1955, 1956 by Warner Bros. Inc. All rights reserved. Used by permission.

*Fool for Love.* Music by George Burt. Reprinted by permission of Go-Glo Music, Inc., and Metro-Goldwyn-Mayer Music Publishing and Soundtracks Department.

*Laura.* Music by David Raksin. Copyright 1944, copyright renewed 1972 by Twentieth Century Fox. Reprinted by permission of CPP/Belwin, Inc., Miami, Fla. All rights reserved.

*The Misfits.* Music by Alex North. Copyright 1974, c/o EMI U Catalog Inc. Reprinted by permission of CPP/Belwin, Inc., Miami, Fla. All rights reserved.

*On the Beach.* Music by Ernest Gold. Copyright 1959 (renewed) by Windswept Pacific Entertainment Co. d/b/a Full Keel Music Co. All rights reserved. Used by permission.

*Separate Tables.* Music by David Raksin. Used by permission of Colby Music Inc., c/o Frendel, Brown & Weissman, New York.

*Sleuth.* Music by John Addison. Copyright 1972 by Twentieth Century Fox. Reprinted by permission of CPP/Belwin, Inc., Miami, Fla. All rights reserved.

*To Kill a Mockingbird.* Music by Elmer Bernstein. Copyright 1963 by Northern Music Corporation, an MCA Company. Copyright renewed. International copyright secured. All rights reserved. Used by permission.

*Tom Horn.* Music by Ernest Gold. Copyright 1980 by Warner Bros. Inc. All rights reserved. Used by permission.

*Tora! Tora! Tora!* Music by Jerry Goldsmith. Copyright 1970 by Twentieth Century Fox. Reprinted by permission of CPP/Belwin, Inc., Miami, Fla. International copyright secured. All rights reserved.

*The Art of Film Music*

*Chapter One*

# The Story's the Thing

At the 1986 Academy of Motion Picture Arts and Sciences awards ceremonies, Alex North was honored with a Lifetime Achievement award. He was the first (and so far the only) composer to receive this award. In his acceptance speech, North said he attempts to meet the "demands and needs of the story conflict and of the interrelationship of the characters involved and, hopefully, to add a personal comment." North was drawing on both his profound talent and insight as a film composer and forty-plus years of experience composing the music for some of the most challenging and significant films of the last few decades. A more succinct definition of the composer's point of view would be hard to come by.

When writing a film score, composers become musical dramatists; their thoughts are on the story and how it is told, as Alex North's comment makes clear. The most distinguished composers possess a genuine theatrical talent and imagination as well as the ability to translate their thoughts into musical sound and gesture. Some have an undeniable instinct that enables them to find the right kind of melodic line, orchestral texture, and musical style to bring out what they intuitively recognize as an essential aspect of a drama. This is a gift. While it takes a great deal of effort, concentration, study, and experience to develop this gift, having it is indispensable to composing for film.

## Music's Vital Role

Most of us can recall instances in which film music tipped the balance, bringing out or amplifying the spirit of the drama. Music has the power to open the frame of reference to a story and to reveal its inner life in a way that could not have been as fully articulated in any other way. In an instant, music can deepen the effect of a scene or bring an aspect of the story into sharper focus. It can have a telling effect on how the characters in the story come across—on how we perceive what they are feeling or thinking—and it can reveal or expand upon subjective aspects and values associated with places and ideas intrinsic to the drama. Further, music being a temporal art, an art that takes place in time (as does film), it can have an enormous impact on the pacing of events, moving things along when needed, dwelling on something that requires attention, accenting this or that instant or event to help bring out the various connections and divergent points of view. In the world of opera, these inherent capabilities of music have been well known for hundreds of years; in film, they are just as fundamental.

Significantly, it is difficult to recall a single feature-length dramatic film—old, new, long, short, traditional, or avant-garde—that does not employ music to dramatic advantage to some extent. Epic films (for example, *Spartacus, Cleopatra, Empire of the Sun*) generally require more music than usual, especially when they contain a preponderance of scenes with broad scope such as landscapes, ceremonies, troop movements, and riots or protests of some sort. In such instances, particularly where dialogue and plot development have been suspended momentarily, music is often needed to maintain a sense of dramatic connection. The same tends to be true of "adventure" films (e.g., *Raiders of the Lost Ark, Star Trek*), in which dialogue gives way to action requiring musical emphasis. Thus, it is the nature of the story and how it is presented on the screen that is a determining factor with respect to the amount of music that is needed. It is telling that while the duration of most feature-length films is between 90 and 120 minutes, up to 30 or 40 minutes of dramatic music is required on average—roughly one-third of the film. This is quite a bit.

Once a story begins, we are principally drawn to what we see on the screen, not what we hear in the music. We have an instinctive inclination toward the human experience, and when we see a person on film we automatically become interested in him or her and in the overall unfolding of the story. The more engaging the drama, the truer this becomes.

Generally, music makes its first appearance during the main (opening) titles, where it is in a position to make substantial comment with lasting effect. Jerry Goldsmith's stirring and penetrative main titles music for *Patton* (1970) (discussed in Chapter 2) is an excellent example. In this instance Goldsmith manages to tell us a great deal about the major character from the outset—his sense of religious conviction and personal commitment to the military—which prepares us for what is to come. The human aspect is, of course, the *sine qua non* of any story. Filmmakers count on music to help bring this out.

## Should Film Music Be Heard?

In concert music the weight of the experience is carried by the music alone. Film music has a much more particularized function, always within a dramatic context. As music in a film is placed here, and then there, but certainly not everywhere, the overall shape or form of a film score becomes a constituent aspect of the film. Certainly, when musical statements are separated by several minutes it is not possible to think in terms of a large-scale musical structure, as we would with concert music or, for that matter, a Mozart opera. Leonard Rosenman points out that "the form is that of the film. What we are dealing with, then, is basically a literary form, not a musical form. Certainly, the music can contribute a great deal in support of an overall shape, but this shape originates with the film itself, not the music." Rosenman adds, "In this sense, it is crucial that a filmmaker has a sense of the larger form, not just a sense of detail."[1]

If the music draws away or diverts from the dramatic shape, line, or impulse, it doesn't fit the film. If it understates the case, it will be a disappointment. And if it overstates a particular situation along the way, it will cause a problem of balance or a distortion of the dramatic line. On the other hand, if the music connects with the film in terms of dramatic shape and meaning, bringing out various aspects in a corroborative manner without overdoing it, the music then begins to fit the film. How this is done in each situation is the basic question—the most important question of all for the film music composer.

Given the importance of the role and function of music in film, it is important to ask to what extent film music is consciously heard generally, or, to put it another way, to what extent it should be heard. David Raksin, one of the most distinguished and experienced film composers, holds the view that "the purpose of film music is not to be noticed for itself. Its great usefulness is the way in which it performs its role without an intervening conscious act of perception. It is most telling when the music registers upon us in a quiet way, where we don't know it's actually happening."[2] Though music enters the plot, so to speak, and takes certain unique technical, aesthetic, and dramatic values into full account, it rarely assumes a commanding position that we are aware of for any length of time. However, this is not to say that the music is not heard or that it is not meant to be heard. Take the music away and we immediately sense its absence, particularly if the music tells us something that needs to be said. As we shall see, there are various situations where film music becomes more noticeable than at other times and where, on occasion, it carries the weight of dramatic development.

## The Contrapuntal Aspect

Many writers allude to the contrapuntal relationship between music and film. When music and film are combined, they interact contrapuntally. Interaction is the key aspect: Music has an impact on film, and film on music. Whether or not we are conscious of this, it is through interaction that the full force of their combined effect comes into play.

In music, the word *counterpoint* is applied to situations involving two or more lines, where each line has a sense of independence or integrity of its own. When combined, they make a statement that is larger than each of the component parts. In our case, there is no question that because of the fundamental difference between the two media—one is visual, the other aural—each is inevitably perceived as having an independence of its own. When placed together to achieve a common goal, a great deal more is expressed than would be possible by means of either medium alone. Indeed, one will heighten the effect of the other.

In music, counterpoint evokes the transfer of attention from one voice to another as an enrichment of the total experience. In string quartets, for instance, primary material passes from the first violin to the viola or the cello and back. This happens in film as well, though to a limited extent. There are occasions when the score takes on a more noticeable role, if only for a short period of time—even a few seconds. This can occur at the beginnings and endings of scenes or at climactic points where dialogue and action come to a momentary pause. Still, this momentary transfer of attention in no way mitigates our preoccupation with what is on the screen. Under the best of circumstances, it substantiates what is on the screen by filling in where dramatic extension is required.

Musical counterpoint traditionally involves the technique of "contrary motion" (two lines moving in opposite directions) as a viable means of achieving linear independence and enlarging upon an overall musical gesture. In a curious manner, this principle emerges in film and music, particularly with regard to the emotional shape of a scene. Imagine a character in a film gradually losing control of a situation and becoming infuriated. In musical terms, we might associate this rise in intensity with the high point of the melodic line. However, a musical gesture or line in the score could just as well be taken in the "opposite" direction, ending on a low pitch as the person screams. The dramatic implication here, underscored by the music, is that the person or the situation has somehow bottomed out, that the crux of the matter has come into full view, or that a point of no return has been reached. This technique has been used quite often and with effective results, as in *Secret Honor* (1984), at the very end of the picture.

## "Supra Reality"

On a broad level, there is music that more or less goes with what appears on the screen (battle music for a battle), and music that establishes a different kind of reality than what is apparent, what Rosenman calls a "supra reality." For instance, pictures of people running in frantic pursuit of something need not be accompanied by music that also "runs." If the dramatic intent of the scene is to amplify an underlying sense of fulfillment or release, it may be better served by a broadly based, lyrical kind of music. The *raison d'être* of this approach is significant. The music interacts with the intrinsic meaning of the sequence, as distinct from a surface-level meaning; it is addressed to what is implicit within the drama, not to what is explicit (such as the visual action), that is, to what you cannot see but need to think about. You will be particularly aware of the music in such instances, because it tells you something that will make an appreciable difference in your perception of the overall event.

This approach is particularly useful in more dramatically involved situations. These ordinarily consist of several layers of thought, where you have something to work with in terms of multiple meanings. For instance, consider the film *Mission* (1986). The story takes place at a time when the natives in Peru were forced to defend themselves against the onslaught of the conquering Spaniards. For the battle, the score recalls a hymn tune that, from the beginning of the film, is associated with the religious spirit embedded in Peruvian culture. Music that ordinarily would be associated with a fierce battle is put aside in favor of a more astute comment.

Film composers are naturally sensitive to the necessity of writing music that will somehow take notice of an important yet understated or implicit aspect of a scene. It should be noted, however, that music by its very nature is expressive of subjective values. It invariably evokes or suggests something of an implicit nature when combined with a picture. Thus, in most cases, the distinction between explicitly and implicitly related music is to some extent a matter of degree, not an either/or proposition.

### Music as Analogue to Film

There is a limit to how far the notion of counterpoint can be taken in the matter of music and film, certainly if all conditions surrounding the practice of counterpoint are considered. As viewed within a musical context alone, various aspects of counterpoint are based on assumptions that, strictly speaking, do not apply in the context of combined music and film. For one thing, in music it is assumed that given two voices, for instance, either voice can function as primary or subsidiary. For another thing, and in respect to canons, fugues, and various other imitative forms, a fundamental assumption has always been that the imitative relationship between voices is readily discernible—that is, when a second voice enters with material introduced by the first voice the reiterated material is quickly recognized and a connection quickly made. These qualities of "recognizability" and "connection" are vital to the cohesive force of any imitative formal design.

However, a problem arises in how we perceive the relationship between music and film that all but rules out these assumptions. In combined music and film, one voice—that of film—is of overriding delineation with respect to literary information, drama, and pictures. Another voice—the music—is subtle, abstract, and symbolic. With this difference in mind, could we ever say with assurance that in a given situation the music is primary and the film performs a subsidiary role? I think not. Eisenstein has pointed out that "musical and visual imagery are actually not commensurable through narrowly [defined] representational elements. . . . [T]he relations between the pictures, and the pictures produced by the musical images, are usually so individual in perception and so lacking in concreteness that they cannot be fitted into any strictly methodological regulations."[3]

Additionally, how could we perceive a canon or fugal structure involving both media, in which pictures of one or more persons in a film assume the role of imitative voices in the music? To bring this off—to allow for the "recognizability" factor basic to imitative forms—we would have to assume that on some level there exists a one-to-one correspondence between the two media. That, as Eisenstein indicates, is not a realistic consideration. For that matter, because of the inherent difference between the two media, it is difficult to imagine any music as being in one-to-one correspondence with film. Leonard Rosenman has said, "in general, I think somebody coming out of the cold and seeing a film does not perceive the music as counterpoint in these strict terms; what happens is that the music becomes an analogue to the film, and sometimes vice versa."[4] It is how and to what extent music catches hold of the spirit or meaning of a film and works with or develops this aspect in its own way that is the key issue in how the two media interrelate in contrapuntal terms.

To be sure, traditional imitative forms are used quite frequently in film scores. I am reminded of David Raksin's comment on his music for *Forever Amber* (1947): "There are enough canons in the score to start a minor Balkan uprising!"[5] In Chapter 3, we will look at a fugue in Hugo Friedhofer's score for *Between Heaven and Hell* (1956) that fits a particular scene in the most effective manner imaginable. It is important to recognize, however, that at a certain point contrapuntal forms begin to have a life and momentum of their own. They invite a feeling of predictability, and the ear accepts, even glorifies in, the imitative process. At some point it is not necessary for all accents in the music to be in synchronization with events on the screen. Discrepancies are not a concern; the spirit of the thing carries the shot. In such cases, however, the scene itself has to have a strength of its own. Recently I was writing a cue (that is, music for a particular scene), and about halfway through I saw an opportunity for a five-part non-tonal canon. Delighted with this prospect, I spent the next few hours writing about a dozen measures. Then I played the canon with a videotape of the sequence, only to find that instead of a minor triumph I had succeeded only in writing myself out of the scene. It overpowered the sequence; it didn't work at all and had to be thrown out.

The point here is that imitative musical structures have proven to be of great value in particularized dramatic situations where there is a tacit agreement between the spirit and feeling underlying these forms and the spirit and content of a scene. On this basis, and in regard to all film music, the contrapuntal relationship between the two media in matters of characterization, accent, pacing, and so on begins to have broad and penetrative significance.

## The Associative Power of Music

Obviously, it is not within the power of music to fully identify or represent something all on its own. It cannot evoke a picture of a house or describe a political system, for instance. There is no such thing as music for convertibles or music for a democracy as distinguished from a dictatorship. Music is a subjective art form with its own language and way of communicating. However, it is within the nature of music to allow for associations, no matter how personal or general. These associations become all the more particularized when music is identified with visual images within a dramatic context—when the music is combined with pictures of something in a story. There is no question that when we see pictures and hear music at the same time we invariably make a connection, if only on an unconscious level.

While it is a fact that a picture of something recognizable instantly conveys what that something is, the camera work, framing, and lighting cannot always coalesce our feelings into a directed pattern, especially when focused on inanimate objects. Imagine a small house nestled at the base of a mountainside, smoke coming from the chimney. Who's inside? A family happily getting ready for bed? Or has a murder just taken place? The music here could make quite a difference. The quality and language of music are vital aids in breaking down the objective explicitness of certain pictures where there is a need to redefine them in a way that is consistent with the intentions of the story.

We will encounter other examples throughout the book in which a single musical idea, melodic line, or motive is brought into association with a character. The opening scene from *East of Eden* (1955), for instance: a connection is made, creating an image, and this image becomes irrevocably glued to the main character and his predicament, especially because that music is brought back when that predicament is at issue. There are many times when music in correspondence with pictures of a particular person or place conjures up an image or feeling that has staying power for an entire sequence, if not longer. Thus, the process of association is a key element in what music contributes to the cohesive power of a film.

### Music's Appeal to the Emotions

Elmer Bernstein has said, "Film conspires with your imagination to remove you from your present reality and take you on a freewheeling trip through your unconscious." The same could be said about art and literature. But films are different. When we sit in a darkened theater watching pictures in motion on a large screen, pictures that tell a story, we are somehow transported in a special way, and we participate. Bernstein asks, "What better companion for such a medium than music? Music is, quite possibly, the one most removed from reality. Of all the arts, music makes the most direct appeal to the emotions. It is a non-plastic, non-intellectual communication between sound vibration and spirit. The listener is not generally burdened with a need to ask what it means. The listener assesses how the music made him feel."[6] In Bernard Herrmann's estimation, music becomes a "communicating link between the screen and the audience, reaching out and enveloping all into one single experience."[7]

*Atmosphere*

Ernest Gold says he tries to find a musical "atmosphere" that belongs to that film alone. Doing this, he says, is "like being involved in an adventure of some kind."[8] There are many "classic" film scores that, when heard without the picture, have the power to evoke the essential character of the images for which they were intended. This is due, in part, to the process of association; having grown accustomed to hearing the score with the picture, images from the story appear unbidden to the mind's eye when we hear the music alone. The two components (music and film) are interwoven when the feeling of the music seems to connect with the innermost sense of the story.

*The Man with the Golden Arm* (1955) is an excellent example of how music connects with the feeling or atmosphere of a particular situation. The music is often described as a classic jazz-idiom film score. Yet, composer Elmer Bernstein has flatly maintained that it is not a jazz score per se. Rather, it is a score "in which jazz elements were incorporated toward the end of creating an atmosphere, a highly specialized atmosphere specific to this film." He continues, "There is something very American and contemporary about all the characters and their problems. I wanted a musical element that could speak readily of hysteria and despair, an element that would localize these emotions to our country, to a large city if possible. Ergo—jazz." *The Man with the Golden Arm* is a hard-edged, contemporary American tragedy. And Bernstein notes that his is not a score that "psychoanalyzes the characters, serving up inner brain on the half shell. It is basically a simple score, dealing with a man and his environment."[9]

Alex North faced a similar task in his music for Edward Albee's *Who's Afraid of Virginia Woolf?* (1966). For both the "main titles" and the "moon" cues, North juxtaposed music with a quality of beguiling calm over and against a complex play involving midlife crisis, unfulfilled promise, tedium, and other aspects of the contemporary American experience. We will discuss the "main titles" cue later. For now, the "moon" cue serves as a short example of the way the subjective quality of the music draws on the visual setting to bring out a particularized feeling of a scene and, as an added plus, sets us up for an unexpected shift in dramatic meaning.

The scene opens with "establishing shots" of George and Martha (Richard Burton and Elizabeth Taylor) walking through a college campus on their way home from a faculty party. It is late, the moon is out, and they are feeling their drinks. In this relatively short cue, North highlights two dramatic factors. One is on the surface—the lazy quality of a casual walk home. The other is a deeper, more ethereal quality associated with a quiet, moonlit environment. [*Accomplishing this, the music rocks gently between two disparate complex harmonies: an A♭ chord with a seventh, ninth, and eleventh and a C-major diatonic cluster with G as the fundamental pitch. The result is two alternating chords with almost entirely different pitch content, further differentiated through means of spacing, tessitura, and orchestration. The A♭ harmony is stated softly by flutes and clarinets in the low register, always accompanied by a three-note motivic fragment from the "main titles" music, played by the celesta. In contrast, the harmonic cluster based on G is scored for muted strings in an extremely high register, along with harp glissandi. The harmonic function of these two entities comes into focus at the end of the cue, where the alternating A♭ and G harmonies finally resolve to C (as in a ♭VI–V–I harmonic progression).*]

The continuous alternation of harmonies in this cue results in a feeling of ambivalence where time—as gauged by a clock—is momentarily suspended. More important, the tentative quality of the moment has a dramatic effect on what follows, which is an abrupt shift to reality. As soon as the music ceases, Martha lets out a bone-chilling cackle and accuses George of being a "terrible cluck." George attempts to calm her, and the drama takes off. (See Ex. I.1.)

*Comedic Tone*

Finding just the right musical feeling for comedy presents another kind of challenge, and a difficult one. This is especially true in a scenario that carries literary implications and ideas beyond the broader comedic sensibilities. A case in point is *Sleuth* (1972), directed by Joseph Mankiewicz and based on Anthony Shaffer's play. The story, a comedy/mystery with a surprise ending, is brilliant, funny, eccentric, and bizarre.

*Sleuth* opens with the main titles superimposed over shots of miniature stage sets, toys, and other bric-a-brac, establishing the element of eccentricity. As the plot unfolds, and the confrontation between Wykes (Laurence Olivier) and Milo (Michael Caine) deepens, this element becomes more and more important to the story. Despite this, or more likely because of and in opposition to it, the composer, John Addison, created an overture for main titles music that instantly imposes a decisive comedic tone. Addison describes the approach behind his decision: "At the beginning of the picture, it was essential not to give away anything that was going to happen. I didn't want to use the themes for the play's characters in the main titles music, yet we had to come up with some kind of idea. What I did was write an overture for a theater production; in the course of it, you hear

Ex. I.1.                    *Who's Afraid of Virginia Woolf?*

## Moon

Alex North

different textures and types of music, almost summing up the different sounds you get in light theatrical music. In a funny way, this effectively tied up with the music in the film to give it an unusual flavor."[10]

Addison's approach, and the way it was carried out, ingeniously establishes a special ambience. The overture has the effect of a real curtain-raiser in the theater, suggesting that we are about to have a good time. To bring this about, Addison deliberately orchestrates the music so that it sounds like a pit orchestra. About this, Addison says, "I could have had as big an orchestra as I wanted, but I purposely made it a little short on the strings, with not quite enough brass and so on, to give the music that pit orchestra feeling.  You never get as many people in the orchestra as you would like in the theater."[11] The formal design of the main titles music and the tonal and melodic means by which it is executed combine to form a turn-of-the-century model of a light theater overture. The effect of light theater is preferred to classical development, and the resulting ambience establishes a buffer for what is to follow in the film.

[*The piece is in rondo form (ABACA), with both introduction and coda. Intervening bridge passages, memorable in character but not repeated, help throw the rondo design into relief (measures 20–26, 34–46, and 63–74) and reflect a kind of buoyant overflow of ideas. The principal sections of the rondo are all in the tonic key; the avoidance of the large-scale tonal shift steers the music away from classical intent and keeps it within the light theatrical style. The previously mentioned bridge passages tonicize different scale degrees, but only briefly. The piece as a whole is constructed of contrasting melodic ideas that bear little relation to each other. These touches, combined with a sprightly orchestration (including deliberate errors in voice-leading, such as the direct octaves in measure 5), provide much of the overture's humorous character. (See Ex. I.2)*].*

Ex. I.2.                                    *Sleuth*

## Main Title

John Addison

In summary, the story is the fundamental issue in film. We are dealing with a literary, not a musical, form. While music has a secondary role in the overall scheme, this role is a vital one. Music and film interact contrapuntally, and this interaction results in a larger statement than would be possible with one or the other medium alone. There is music that follows what is apparent on the screen, and music that is suggestive of something that is not apparent, a "supra reality." However, most music does both; its subjective nature and uniqueness of language makes this so. It is, finally, a matter of degree.

While music is unable to describe something, it does allow for associations, particularly when combined with pictures. Music appeals to our emotions. It can tell us something about somebody, and it certainly can contribute to our sense of the ambience or atmosphere of a given situation.

These considerations are basic to the study of film music and lead quite naturally to the question of characterization.

## Chapter Two

# Characterization

The most crucial and most difficult problem a film composer faces is finding the music that seems absolutely right for both a film and its characters. Even subtle melodic, harmonic, or rhythmic changes in the music, not to mention the orchestration, can make an enormous difference in achieving a sense of "rightness." Composers can recall times when the right sound or gesture occurred to them immediately after they had seen the film the first time. They can just as readily recollect days of agonizing revisions before hitting upon that magical connection in which the music is irrevocably "glued" to images on the screen.

Film music can connect either with individual characters or with groups of people. In so doing, the music responds to the meanings behind various actions and interactions. On occasion, it is important for music to connect with meanings of a symbolic nature that transcend the surface meaning of dialogue and action. Generally, overall meanings become apparent through shifts in emotions over a long time span. Music that corroborates these shifts ties in with the overall dramatic presentation of the story.

Unlike the theater, film can move easily and rapidly through time and space. In *The Boys from Brazil* (1978), for instance, the story begins in Vienna and then instantly leaps to Paraguay. Flashbacks in *The Spirit of St. Louis* (1957) take us not only to different places but also to different times. The story of *2001: A Space Odyssey* (1968) progresses from the prehistoric past to the future. Music is particularly adept at establishing an aura that is identified with a time and place, thus rendering these cuts more plausible. In all the above, music functions in a characterizational capacity.

17

## Individual People

Ernest Gold describes the problem of getting the right feeling in the music for an individual character: "It is important that music is neither more profound nor more superficial than the character actually is. If you take a person with great dignity, it is all too easy to trivialize him; conversely, you can take a very trivial person and make him absolutely ludicrous by giving him a presence, a depth of feeling, or a power of appearance which isn't and shouldn't be there. This is one of the least tangible aspects of film scoring, and very difficult."[1]

These are extreme cases. The more subtle situations require concentrated thought. This procedure is complicated, says Gold, because "a composer will measure the movie character that he scores a little bit by his own reactions, so that in a way he is writing about himself and how he would react to a given situation. This is one reason that a composer will write a score one way, another composer will do something slightly different, and both scores could be equally suitable, equally valid, and equally good."[2]

### Mental Processes

Hugo Friedhofer, a giant in film music, had an uncanny gift for striking just the right balance for the characters in a given situation. He once observed that "music is capable of portraying the mental processes of the actor, which motivate him to do such and such."[3] Two scenes in Friedhofer's score for *The Young Lions* (1958) illustrate this point.

*The Young Lions* takes place in World War II. In one sequence, Marlon Brando, a German officer on leave, delivers a gift to his captain's wife, Gretchen, a seductress who harbors little concern for her husband. She invites Brando to spend the evening with her. For this scene, Friedhofer composed a jazz-like waltz that initially appears as source music coming from the phonograph. Written in a style reminiscent of Kurt Weill, the music is angular and tonally deceptive. These qualities instantly fuse with the provocative character of the woman, all of which has a commanding effect on Brando. A four-measure introduction for bass clarinet, horns, and vibraphone establishes a casual feeling. However, it is the melody stated by the alto saxophone (measure 4) that makes the point: In a beguiling manner, it moves through a circuitous harmonic progression with apparent ease and grace. It avoids large intervalic leaps, and its breezy melodic contour fits and indeed enlarges upon both the situation and her enticing qualities. Then, at measure 24, Friedhofer writes a soaring bridge passage for the violins and cellos (in octaves) that takes on a pleading quality, leading both the music and the scene forward. The situation produces conflicting emotions for Brando's stoic character (Christian), but the music ties in with the effect Gretchen wants to have on him. (See Ex. II.1.)

Ex. II.1.                              *The Young Lions*

# The Captain's Lady

**Hugo Friedhofer**

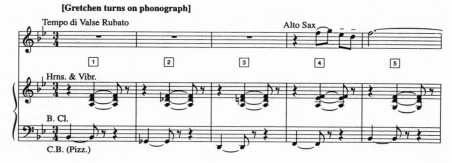

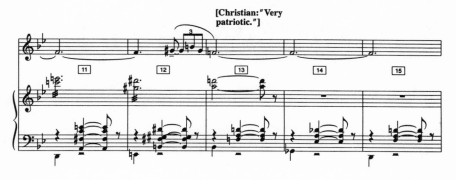

*(continued)*

*(continued)*

[Gretchen: "Welcome to
Germany, soldier."]

[Gretchen places a
veil over her hair]

[She admires herself
in the mirror]

[Gretchen turns to
face Christian]

In an earlier section of the same film, music is brought in to reveal a different side of Brando's character. In this scene, he appears with Françoise, a young woman for whom he develops an abiding affection. Scored for full orchestra, the music connects with, and builds on, Brando's exuberance, which is generally hidden by his controlled demeanor. Diatonic progressions are preferred to the angular, chromatic shifts employed in the other scene, and the effect is less complicated and more forthright. Especially moving is the high point of the melodic line, which begins with measure 13. Pushed forward harmonically through a circle of fifths, the music here emphasizes a deeper level of feeling and openness that is not so apparent on the screen as it perhaps should be to make the point. (See Ex. II.2.)

Ex. II.2.                    *The Young Lions*

## Christian and Françoise

Hugo Friedhofer

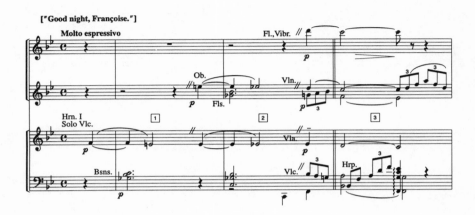

["Good night, Françoise."]

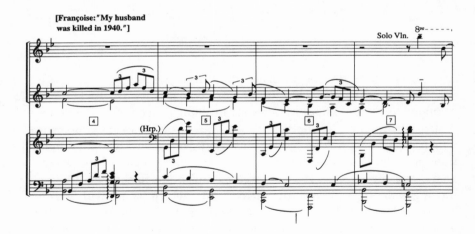

[Françoise: "My husband
was killed in 1940."]

*(continued)*

*(continued)*

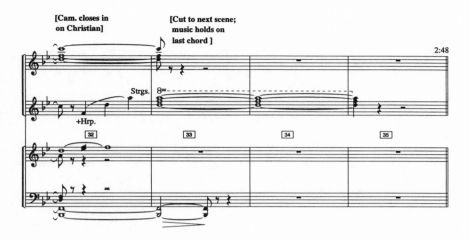

There are countless instances where the precise choice of musical style and instrumentation plays a very significant role in the way an individual character comes across. For example, to close off the opening scene of *Sleuth*, John Addison chose an effective Baroque-style music for harpsichord. The film opens with Laurence Olivier, who plays a detective novelist, animatedly dictating a passage for his next book. Addison says, "The idea I had for Olivier was to use a harpsichord playing a single line along with a limited number of other instruments. I was initially worried about this, but a film editor helped me to appreciate why this was right. What it had to do with was the mind of the writer (Olivier), who was rather an intellectual and mathematical type; Baroque writing, with harpsichord, seemed to convey this in some strange way. In other places within the picture, where I combine the harpsichord with 'misterioso' effects, the approach again works very well, and adds a touch of humor."[4] (See Ex. II.3.)

Ex. II.3.                    *Sleuth*

## Sleuth Theme

John Addison

*(continued)*

*(continued)*

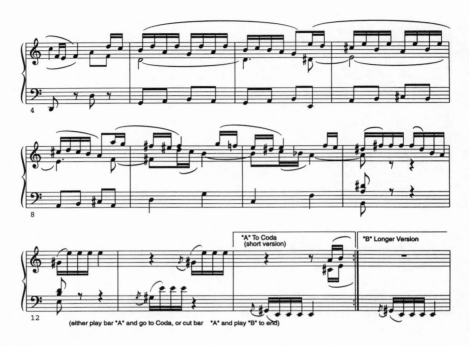

(either play bar "A" and go to Coda, or cut bar   "A" and play "B" to end)

In the first scene of *East of Eden,* Leonard Rosenman is quick to identify and focus on an essential element of the narrative that connects with the major character's—Cal, played by James Dean—introverted personality and his yearning to know his mother. Rosenman points out that by contrast, "the main titles theme is very simple, like a folk tune. Toward the end there is a transition to the first cue, which goes into the inner life of Dean's character, which is psychological. At this point there is a difference in style, which leans toward Expressionism, and a difference in the orchestration, which involves smaller combinations of instruments and solo."[5]

This scene begins with a shot of Cal sitting on a curb. A woman passes behind him. Glancing up, he decides to follow her. We have no notion why—not yet, anyway. But the music immediately establishes a frame of reference by saying something about Cal's character.

The music is brought in as Cal enters the frame of the first shot. [*An arpeggiation of fourths opens into a sustained chord in the brass, accenting her appearance. As the camera cuts to Cal, the pitches are transferred to the strings, presenting a softer sound, with the harp settling on a repeated C-natural (measure 2).*] When the woman passes behind Cal (measure 3), the clarinet introduces the first two notes of an important and memorable five-note motive, which is stated in full when Cal finally turns to look at her (measure 4); this motive is extended as Cal watches the woman walk down the street (measures 6–7). The troubled expression on his face and the five-note motive become associated with a yearning he holds in private. Reference to a motivic idea is a powerful way of making a connection between a character and a prevailing emotion. Significantly, the motive is brought back in various guises throughout the picture when this aspect of Cal's sense of longing is an issue.

The cue is rounded off by a descending figure in thirds (measure 8), antithetically related to the opening of the cue as the woman walks toward the camera in the closing shot. Cal is now in the background. (See Ex. II.4.)

Ex. II.4.                    *East of Eden*

**Leonard Rosenman**

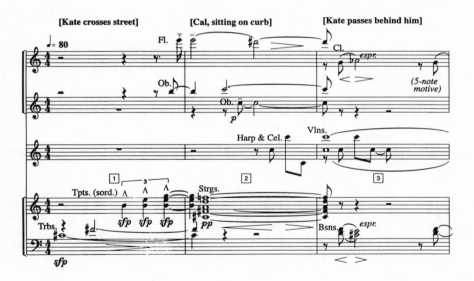

(continued)

*(continued)*

(var. of 5-note motive)

Musical syntax or mode of construction exists as an additional means to reveal or corroborate the nature of an individual's mental process. Toward the end of *Cross Creek* (1986), there is a long scene in which music is needed to illuminate as well as dramatize the process one goes through when coming to a critical decision. In the "rowboat" scene, which is perhaps the climax of the picture, the main character mulls over her situation in order to decide what to do next. There is no dialogue. The music, composed by Leonard Rosenman, moves in one direction, hesitates, and then moves in another direction. In some way it tells us what she is thinking and how she is going about it. It is obvious she is dealing with certain ambiguities in her life. When she finally reaches a decision, Rosenman arrives at a six–four chord that prepares for a statement of an extended thematic idea.

In many instances, composers have employed a single melodic line to connect with a character. In the opening of *Death of a Salesman* (1983), for example, Alex North introduces a theme for solo alto flute in the low to middle register as Willy Loman (Dustin Hoffman) laboriously removes sample cases from his car and carries them to his house. With this theme, the full weight of Willy's loneliness (in contrast to his persona) comes into focus. Significantly, playwright Arthur Miller has on many occasions publicly thanked Alex North for bringing out the multidimensional quality of Willy's character (in his music for the original play and both film versions), a character that has become an icon in American theater. (See Ex. II.5.)

Ex. II.5.                          *Death of a Salesman*

**Alex North**

## Groups of People

In each of the preceding examples, the music is directed toward the characterization of an individual. But there are times when music must deal with a collective point of view, involving more than just one or two people. Situations emerge that have a governing influence on *groups* of people, situations that lie at the heart of a thematic problem. In *Sweet Smell of Success* (1957), for instance, all the characters are immersed in a psychologically agonizing and violent urban society. In much the same style as that used in *The Man with the Golden Arm,* Elmer Bernstein wrote deliberately macho music that was purposely overstated and that ultimately underscores the vulnerability and sterility that the main characters make every effort to hide.

Leith Stevens had a similar task for *The Wild One* (1954), a story that takes place in the 1950s. Music was required to identify and state a collective persona and point of view. Stevens says, "The characters in the play are young people, full of tensions, for the most part inarticulate and, though exhibitionistic, confused and wandering. These characteristics suggested the use of progressive jazz or bop (call it what you will) as an important aspect of the score. This music, with its nervous searching quality, seemed best to complement those characters."[6] Producer Stanley Kramer and director Laszlo Benedek consulted with Stevens while working on the shooting script before the film was made. In this fashion they were able to count on the implicit nature of the music to help carry various shots without resorting to extraneous dialogue—which would have been anathema to the characters in the story. Here is a case where the predetermination of music for a film had an effect on the actual writing and shooting.

In many of the epic films about World War II, the scenarios revolve around massive numbers of men and women. As a result of surrounding circumstances, these large groups generally require differentiating musical treatment. Such is the case in the monumental *A Bridge Too Far* (1977). The battle scenes were shot with such extraordinary realism that music was rarely needed. Sound effects alone often work more effectively in such cases. In other scenes, composer John Addison decided to use music to bring out distinctive emotional values associated with large groups of people. Addison says, "The way this worked out was that we had three themes. One theme was associated with the Dutch Resistance—people who, as the battle began, thought they would be liberated and were overjoyed, having been oppressed by the Nazi regime for five or six years. Their cities had been destroyed and many of their band captured by the Germans and taken to concentration camps. Another theme was associated with the airborne forces, and a third with the armored forces."[7] That Addison was particularly sensitive to the distinction between the latter two groups is due to his having served as a tank commander in an armored division in the very battles depicted in the film. One can easily understand, in that light, why the stirring march that characterizes the armored forces has such a distinctly positive edge. (See Ex. II.6.)

Ex. II.6.                    *A Bridge Too Far*

## Armored Forces Theme

John Addison

(continued)

*(continued)*

## Symbolic Meanings

Film music is sometimes called upon to signify certain ideas. Though music cannot do this on its own, it can, as we discussed in Chapter 1, allow for associations. Consider the relatively straightforward examples of the recruitment documentaries and newsreels of World War II. Soldiers were shown preparing for and being transported to battle, usually with the accompanying music written in a George M. Cohan Broadway musical style. The music symbolized the spirit of eagerness to serve one's country and, as an added plus, served to downplay any fears of being wounded, more so of being killed. Stirring music written in this style had an effect upon the audiences of the period and, for the moment, eased the pain and apprehension of going to war. Many feature films of the same era employed a similar musical approach, and for the same reasons.

Signifying symbolic meanings is an important function of film music. There are times when a single musical idea within a given style has been used to tie up diverse elements. What may exist as a seemingly insurmountable problem for the composer can develop into an opportunity. In the book *Film World,* author Ivor Montague tells of an experience that illustrates this point. Montague, in a hotel with free time on his hands, turned on the television and began to watch, in sequence, "the burning of the Reichstag, the capture of Van der Lubbe, the trial of the accused and a football match." But, quite by accident, he had turned on the volume control to the radio instead of the TV and was listening to musical excerpts from a Viennese comic opera. Unaware of his error, he says he was amazed at "how well the music seemed to capture a particular meaning of the visuals."[8] The overblown pompousness and seriocomic tone of the Viennese waltzes apparently said something curiously revealing about each of the sequences, and, strangely enough, the sequences seemed to be bound together, sharing a common point of view.

There are numerous examples in which music has been called upon to bring things together. For the "Raindrop" sequence in *Butch Cassidy and the Sundance Kid* (1968), director George Roy Hill wanted to establish a special bond between Etta Place (Katharine Ross) and Butch (Paul Newman), and to make the alliance between them and Sundance (Robert Redford) more understandable. In *Film Music Notebook* Hill writes, "Dialogue wouldn't have been good because it wasn't that kind of relationship. So we created a scene and used the music specifically for that purpose. That was where music was able to do something I wouldn't have been able to with dialogue."[9] Burt Bacharach was commissioned to write a tender yet playful song to be used against shots of Newman and Ross riding a bicycle outside their house/hideaway. There was no dialogue or sound effects.

*Irony*

In some cases, composers have found it necessary to write music that symbolizes the ironic nature of an entire film. In the decidedly complex *Who's Afraid of Virginia Woolf?,* Alex North had to uncover the underlying meaning of a psychologically violent play, a meaning that could be expressed in musical terms. The main characters (George and Martha) are virtually at each other's throats for the duration of the film. Their lives are so intertwined and enmeshed that each is caught in the web of the other, and together they thrash around in disappointment, frustration, and anger. Despite this, North saw a love relationship, albeit a self-consuming one, that was central to the symbolic if not ironic meaning of the play. The main titles music introduces a quiet lyricism in direct juxtaposition to the explosive nature of the dialogue. This music is used in varied forms throughout the film as a reminder that, at bottom, the couple have a powerful affection for and attraction to each other. (See Ex. II.7.)

Ex. II.7.  *Who's Afraid of Virginia Woolf?*

## Prelude (Main Title)

Alex North

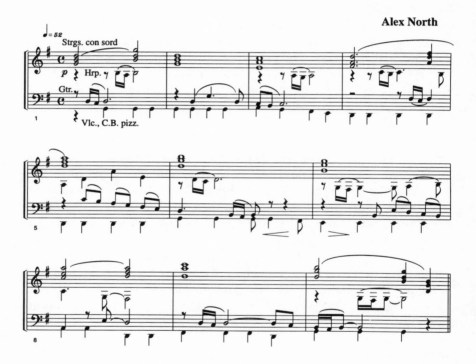

The question of irony comes up time and time again and presents unique opportunities for music. For instance, in *Al Capone* (1959), there is a sequence based on a contradiction between an action and the context in which it occurs. In this sequence, Capone steps into a flower shop to buy a wreath for Big Jim's funeral, and within seconds the scene dissolves to Capone at the funeral. Even though it was he who had Big Jim murdered, it was necessary for him to attend the funeral to publicly present a posture of innocence. David Raksin was thus confronted with the task of writing funeral music that was somber and at the same time betrayed the violence of the assassination. (See Ex. II.8a.)

Ex. II.8a.                              *Al Capone*

## Cortege of MacDuff

David Raksin

*(continued)*

(continued)

[*The opening gesture of this cue occurs quite frequently throughout the film, mainly in association with the violent side of Capone's nature. Indeed, it is a principal motive in the score. On the dissolve to the funeral, beginning with measure 3, the trombones are given a complex (almost Straussian) chromatic harmonic progression over a* G#-D# *pedal that moves*

(continued)

toward an altered V7 of C$^\#$ (on the shot of the hearse door), measure 7. This is soon followed by a series of third-related altered seventh chords from G$^\#$-B-D and F in the bass, ending on D$^\flat$, as a possible resolution of the G$^\#$, enharmonically notated. The jagged, rhythmic punctuations in 6/8 meter, given to the lower clarinets, fourth trombone, and percussion, create a

*(continued)*

:30 1/3

[Casket thumps
against inner wall
of hearse]

dramatically needed sense of imbalance that contrasts with the insistent funereal plodding of
the upper line in 2/4 meter, as stated by B♭ clarinets and horns. Still, the somber quality of
the scene remains intact and this is due, in part, to the orchestration: all winds in their lower
register —no strings. (See Ex. II.8b.)]

Ex. II.8b.                          *Al Capone*

**David Raksin**

## Archetypes

The sense of irony resides, more often than not, in our identifications with well-known archetypal figures. Al Capone in movies has become an archetype of the gangster. Another type in our culture is the ubiquitous western hero. A portrait of calm control, he stands for many qualities. As we have come to know him, he is generally responsible for his actions and, while quick on the trigger, moves only when necessary. Typically, his background, plans, goals, and life are left unexplored. He never talks about any of that. He is the man of the present.[10]

The principle of honor, as seen in *Tom Horn* (1980), has uncompromising results that exist on the edge of irony. In this film, Steve McQueen portrays Tom Horn, the western hero whose arrival in a small town at the turn of the century does not go unnoticed. His archetypal qualities are instantly recognizable: He is deliberate, accountable, surprising in his quickness, and nonverbal. These qualities prove to be just as much a liability as an asset. A ranch owner hires him to ward off a group of cattle rustlers, but once the job is done the townspeople turn on him and, alleging ruthlessness, bring a trumped-up charge of murder against him. The purity of his archetypal honor does not allow Tom to defend himself, and he is eventually convicted and hanged. (This, by the way, was one of Steve McQueen's last movies, and his maturity in the role is evident.)

In his excellent score for *Tom Horn,* Ernest Gold gives just the right sense of character and direction to the central figure. Gold says he spent more than a week composing the main titles music, as he had planned to derive most of the remaining score from the opening. He points out that "the problem was that it was essentially a one-character picture, and this suggested a monothematic approach based on a relatively long thematic idea." The principal theme is somewhat unyielding and thus corresponds with the stoic quality of Tom's character. [*It is constructed with perfect intervals (fourths and fifths), accompanied by diatonic harmonies with modal implications over an extended pedal point in the bass.*] The end titles (after Tom has been executed) present the theme more lyrically. As Gold says, "This is what I was aiming for from the beginning."[11] His approach in the music helped substantiate the central meaning of the film—that honor can persist as clearly in defeat as in victory. (See Ex. II.9.)

Another archetypal figure that plays heavily in our culture is that of the soldier. *Patton* comes to mind. For this picture, Jerry Goldsmith's main titles music not only establishes a symbolic edge but also joins past with present. He achieves this by bringing out at least three aspects of the main character. To be specific, the triplet figures for trumpets rever-

Ex. II.9.                    *Tom Horn*

## Main Titles

**Ernest Gold**

berate in the distance, echoing past battles. It is later revealed that Patton had a deep-seated belief in reincarnation; a powerful diatonic hymn in counterpoint to the trumpet figures suggests a religious dimension of his character. Patton is also characterized in the score as the quintessential soldier, a man of action who was born to lead. The famous march, first introduced lightly by a piccolo, then taken up by the horns and eventually by the full orchestra, corresponds to this notion. One senses Patton's strength and invulnerability—characteristics that have long-range symbolic implications in the drama.

The soldier is also seen in a collective sense. The main titles music for *The Best Years of Our Lives* (1946) serves as an excellent example. An opening fanfare-like gesture prepares for, and is immediately followed by, the *Best Years* theme. The broad, settled quality of the theme, created by triad unfolding melodic shapes and root position diatonic harmonies, is associated throughout the film with moments where the three principals are viewed as a "collective hero"—a larger-than-life point of view in the story. [*In a space-opening gesture, the main titles music begins with the statement of two minor thirds (x) separated by a far-reaching octave, followed by a cadential progression (y) to C major rather than C minor, as might be expected. (See Ex. II.10.)*]

Ex. II.10.            *The Best Years of Our Lives*

## Main Titles

**Hugo Friedhofer**

While the film relates both the strengths and the weaknesses that its characters possess, along with the odds they are up against and the way they deal with them, the *Best Years* theme and its attendant cadential progression are used throughout to shore up the symbolic notion that while men are faulty, Man is noble. The *Best Years* score, by Hugo Friedhofer, is considered one of the finest ever written for film. (See Ex. II.11a, b.)

Ex. II.11a.                    *The Best Years of Our Lives*

## Main Titles Theme

**Hugo Friedhofer**

Ex. II.11b.

*Point of View and Musical Style*

The style of the music is itself capable of making a symbolic statement about the drama and the characters involved. In general, musical style reflects a point of view: classicism, romanticism, expressionism, impressionism, and so on. On a more personal level, a style can be brought into congruence with the nature or disposition of a particular character, and it will speak volumes about that character and his or her role in the film. The music for *To Kill a Mockingbird* (1962) is a splendid example of this.

The focus of attention in *To Kill a Mockingbird* is on Atticus, the father and small-town lawyer. Resolute, thoughtful, and articulate, he is a person whose words and deeds command attention. However, the story is told from a child's point of view by Atticus's grown-up daughter. If the music had picked up on an adult version, as would be associated with Atticus, a conflict in perspective and style would have necessarily resulted. The problem Elmer Bernstein faced in determining an approach to the score is this: On the one hand, there was the seriousness of the drama, which involved racism, alleged rape, murder, and the type of insanity that precipitates and follows these situations. On the other hand, there were the little girl's words, phrases, and memories, which echoed the events as she saw them.

The child's point of view could easily have been overwhelmed by a weighty musical style and commentary.

Bernstein found an answer in his landmark score by tying the dichotomous elements together. He discarded the possibility of what would ordinarily be taken as children's music. Instead, he opted for a "child's adult music"[12]—music with the sophistication of the adult world, which retained the charm and unrefined elegance of a child's world. (See Ex. II.12.)

Ex. II.12.                     *To Kill a Mockingbird*

## Main Titles Theme

**Elmer Bernstein**

*(continued)*

*(continued)*

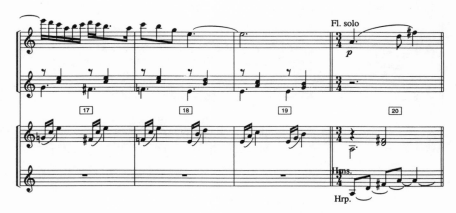

[*The passage from* Mockingbird *contains many sophisticated elements. The flute solo in the first four measures seems innocent enough, but a subtle durational change on the pitch B (first note of measure 11) causes a meter change, from 4/4 to an asymmetrical 5/4. The ostinato figure in the clarinet and harp accompaniment creates a light background effect, with the clarinet notes in 16ths and the harp in 16th-note triplets, in a 2 to 3 ratio. Harmonically, the accompaniment, including the violas, combines to form the first inversion of an F-major seventh chord (with added augmented eleventh—the B-natural again), suggestive of the Lydian mode, while the melody in the flute tends to outline an E-minor triad. The result is a linearly unfolding superimposition of different chordal structures, or polydiatonicism. In the 6/8 measures that follow, the piano presents a secondary thematic idea having an asymmetrical rhythmic structure within itself, as it divides into three measures, then four.*]

Considering its complexity, one might well question Bernstein's description of this as a "child's adult music." But looking at it from a fresh perspective, one sees that the thematic material occupies the range of only an octave, the range of a child's voice. The orchestration is of further significance. Employing a small ensemble consisting of flutes, clarinets, harp, and violas, Bernstein works within a transparent texture that produces an inherently soft sound. The 6/8 section, scored for piano, vibraphone, and celesta alone, is reminiscent of a music box. In short, Bernstein has created a music in a neoclassical style that is at once complex yet, on the surface, beautifully innocent. Accessible at the symbolic level, it is, indeed, real "child's adult music."

Musical styles such as those mentioned earlier are recognizable through reference to attendant harmonic, melodic, and orchestrational practice considered to be characteristic of the style in question. For instance, the expressionistic style ordinarily consists of complex or non-triadic chordal structures along with wide-ranged melodic shapes within a unique but fast-changing orchestrational texture. Dodecaphonic reference (a 12-tone compositional approach) is preferred to traditional tonality. In contrast to a classical style, expressionism tends to place an emphasis on the dramatic importance and difference of each fleeting moment.

A well-known sequence from *On the Beach* (1959) is a good illustration. The music for this sequence draws heavily on the serial or 12-tone approach and it bears a close resemblance to the expressionistic style of writing. Furthermore, and most important, Gold is able to bring out what he regards as the symbolic meaning of the sequence by these means.

In this film, a nuclear weapons exchange has enveloped the earth in deadly radiation clouds. Australia is the last surviving continent. An indecipherable telegraph signal, judged to be coming from the California coast, indicates that someone, somewhere, has survived. A submarine is dispatched to the San Francisco and San Diego bays to make contact with the source of this signal.

As the submarine passes under the Golden Gate Bridge, the first six notes of a twelve-note set (see Ex. II.13a) are stated one after another by brass and woodwinds. This opens up the scene in preparation for what follows: a commanding disjunct thematic line based on a derived set, given to the French horns. This line is followed by statements of a subset played in rapid succession by the keyboard instruments, creating an overall crashing effect of orchestral sound. (See Ex. II.13b.)

Ex. II.13a.  *On the Beach*

Ex. II.13b.                         *On the Beach*

**Ernest Gold**

This music is brought back as we are shown isolated shots of a desolate city through the periscope. The music goes against the character of these shots; one might well expect silence. But the tumultuous sound of the music dramatizes the "supra reality"— the tragedy of a lifeless, once-beautiful city. These periscope shots are intercut with shots of the captain and other members of the crew. For the first few of these, Gold omits music altogether. Their stunned reactions make sufficient statement.

Moments later, a crew member, a native San Franciscan, jumps ship and swims to shore, preferring to die at home rather than wait for death in Australia. The next day he is sighted in a rowboat, and for this scene Gold brings back the twelve-note set, giving it to two oboes in unison playing a repeated-note rhythm vaguely reminiscent of the telegraph signal. The effect provides the ideal touch as the sub gets under way, leaving the young crew member to face his own mortality alone. (See Ex. II.13c.)

Ex. II.13c.                                    *On the Beach*

Although Gold is not a proponent of the 12-tone system, he draws upon elements of this compositional approach in an effort to get at the symbolic aspects of the story. Gold says, "I used the 12-tone set approach in this sequence to bring out the chain reaction of radiation, the billiard balls analogy used in freshman physics. This is precisely where I like the 12-tone system—it is like physics to me. The repeated-note rhythm resembling the telegraph is there because it was important to keep the symbol of the telegraph alive."[13] The mission's real purpose is to discover the origins of the signal.

Mention of the expressionistic style in general and the 12-tone system in particular brings to mind an observation that many theatergoers easily accept music of this genre when at the movies but cannot bear the thought of listening to it in the concert hall, an irony in itself. Before moving on to the next example, I wish to comment on this. There is no question that music associated with the expressionistic point of view or style demands a great deal from the listener. Indeed, the atonal nature of the music poses an immediate problem for anybody whose experience and enjoyment have revolved around tonal or key-related music. However, I suspect that an acceptance of it is much easier at the movies because the audience is not compelled to focus only on the music. As has been said, everybody's attention is on the story, after all, and the story leads the way. It is a different matter in the concert hall.

While atonal music has found its way into countless film scores over the past several decades, very few film composers have drawn upon strict 12-tone compositional procedures. These procedures are generally regarded as too cumbersome for extended theatrical scores. I asked Jerry Fielding about this, and he said, "The twelve-tone system is okay, but if you want to write scales, forget it."[14] The generalized use of the atonal concept, however, is considered particularly effective in certain situations, especially those requiring a relatively high level of musical intensity. Unfortunately, there is a widespread belief that only situations involving cataclysmic events, neurotic behavior, and so on qualify as appropriate occasions for such music. This is troublesome for people who have had positive experiences with atonal musical language. While it is clear that the use of atonality offers the potential for dramatic intensification, many feel discouraged by an insistence that its use be limited to extreme situations.

There is no question that a score involving familiar-sounding melodic and harmonic points of departure and arrival within a tonal construct is, by and large, more compatible with the dramatic meaning, style, and intent of many films, at least at this time. How attitudes toward the use of atonal or other musical languages will develop in the future is for anybody to speculate. The exciting thing is that the musically trained film composers of today have many choices, perhaps more than ever before—a definite plus in the film medium.

In the examples cited from *On the Beach,* the musical process was based on discrete compositional detail within a given musical style. However, in the next example, taken from the main titles of *The Young Lions,* the process is out in the open (though no less complex), and the musical gesture associated with a symbolic meaning is made clear from the outset.

The music for *The Young Lions* begins with a two-measure rhythmic ostinato for percussion, which is repeated over and over again throughout the cue. It is a march-like gesture that has been successfully used in many concert scores (for example, "Mars, The Bringer of War," from Gustav Holst's *The Planets,* and the last movement of Morton Gould's *West Point Symphony*) to connote the essence of power, inevitability, or militarism. (See Ex. II.14.)

Ex. II.14.                    *The Young Lions*

**Hugo Friedhofer**

The *Young Lions* theme, presented during the main titles sequence, is given to brass instruments beginning with measure 5. The sheer weight of the theme and of the orchestration makes a statement that transcends personal characterization. In one sense, it is in direct contrast to the personal side of any of the characters and instead is addressed to a spirit of unyielding determination on a broad level. Its decisiveness springs from its melodic shape and the way in which it is harmonized. (See Ex. II.15.)

Ex. II.15.                    *The Young Lions*

## Main Titles Theme

Hugo Friedhofer

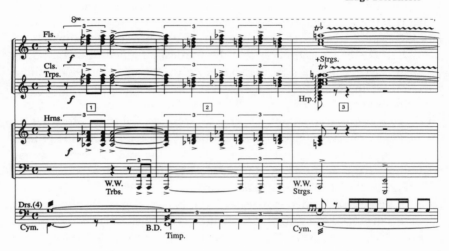

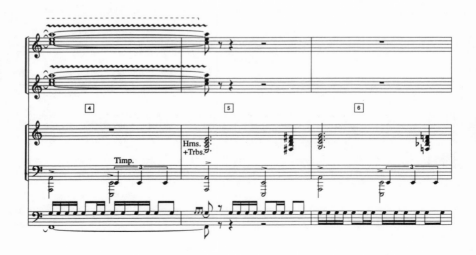

W.W.
Strgs.

Cym.

Cym.

*(continued)*

*(continued)*

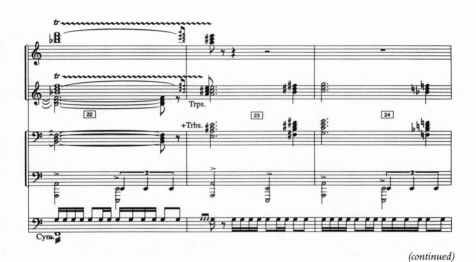

*(continued)*

*(continued)*

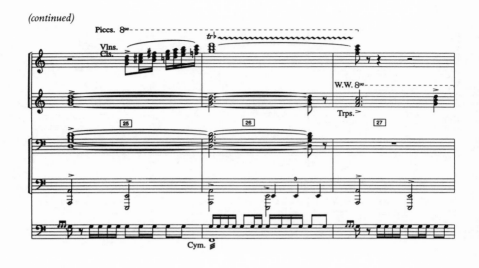

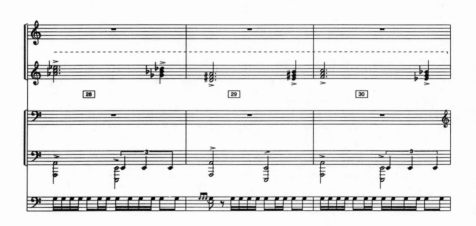

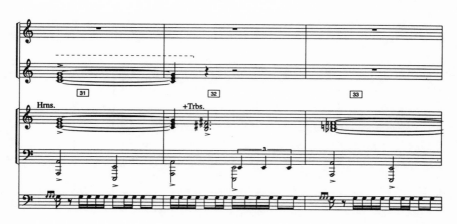

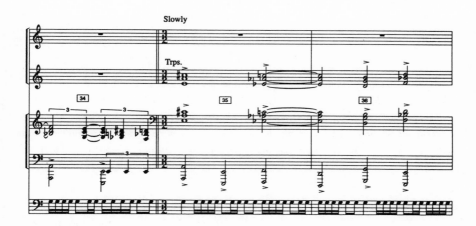

*(continued)*

*(continued)*

[*Certain pitches predominate at departure and arrival points within local designs. For in-stance, the top line in measures 5–8 moves from E to G, and instead of moving onward, it returns to E. This becomes a characteristic melodic design serving the whole piece. This design is made all the more insistent by the harmony, consisting of triads in parallel motion. The following analytical sketch reveals the underlying harmonic structure. (See Ex. II.16.)*]

Ex. II.16.                    *The Young Lions*

**Hugo Friedhofer**

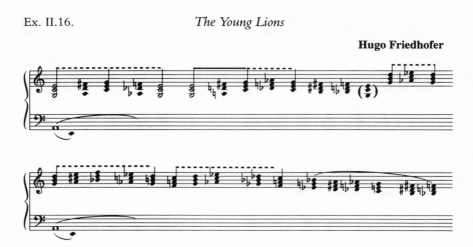

### The Danger of Confusion in Point of View

The musical dramatization of a symbol is a subtle matter, albeit a viable function of film music. At the same time there are dangers in entrusting music with a symbolic responsibility. One danger lies in the potential confusion of identification.

For music to have its intended effect, it must be clear whose cause it singles out. Kracauer, in his book *Theory of Film,* observes that, in Pudovkin's *The Deserter* (1933), "the gloomy pictures of a demonstration of defeated workers are synchronized with an uplifting music, which he [Pudovkin] inserted with the firm conviction that it would drive home the unbroken fighting spirit of the defeated, and make the audience anticipate their ultimate triumph."[15] Kracauer points out that the uplifting music could well have been identified with the feelings of the temporary victors—that is, the employers—and thereby caused confusion as to whose cause was being celebrated.

### The Problem with Quotations

Another source of difficulty stems from the well-known technique of using musical quotations to identify the nature of a situation. Kracauer points out that "a few bars of Mendelssohn's Wedding March suffices to inform the spectator that he is watching a wedding." But, as Kracauer warns us, these same few bars can "remove from his [the spectator's] consciousness all visual data which do not directly bear on that ceremony or conflict with his preconceived notions of it."[16] In other words, if other thoughts, ideas, or actions are of greater importance to the narrative than those that directly bear on the wedding itself, then the decision to bring in the "Wedding March" should be reconsidered.

Musical quotations of national anthems have been used to delineate national pride. While these quotations can be effective on certain occasions, they (like the "Wedding March") are usually so well known they can distract from the uniqueness of a particular dramatic situation by invoking extraneous associations. Experienced composers are sensitive to this problem. Take the case of the Bogart classic *Casablanca* (1942). Max Steiner's score is sprinkled with fragments of "La Marseillaise," "Deutschland über Alles," and "Die Wacht am Rhein." Steiner, instinctively aware of the pitfalls inherent in their use, avoids extended quotations for the most part and prefers, instead, to use motivic statements of three or four notes (used primarily to help articulate scene beginnings and endings), wherein the themes are not overly dominant. Steiner's score goes beyond the use of certain known thematic ideas as ambient quotation technique. While they are an integral part of the picture, so is the presence of the song "As Time Goes By." The score draws heavily upon references to this tune and uses it as an important piece of source music.[17]

### The Risk of Overstatement

Alan Downer has said that "films are given to symbolic imagery." In his article about John Huston, Downer points to several beautifully constructed scenes that are undeniably symbolic. In *The Red Badge of Courage* (1951), for instance, "the charge is interrupted by a head and shoulders view of a soldier kneeling, fumbling for his lost glasses, finding them, hooking them carefully over his ears and then collapsing in death. A completely cinematic—wordless—presentation of the theme."[18]

Downer goes on to say that "symbolism is always a threat to film art. Even *The Maltese Falcon* (1941), ruthlessly realistic as it may be, ends with a close-up of Mary Astor, prison-bound, as the iron bars of an elevator door close across her face. And perhaps the empty bag of gold caught in the cactus plant at the end of *The Treasure of the Sierra Madre* (1948) is a symbolic statement."[19]

The problem is that it is easy to make the symbol into an overstatement. And this is where composers must be very careful. Music that identifies with a symbolic image could push the matter to the point at which the expressive power of the image is suddenly reduced. If actors are involved, overly dramatic music for these tentative moments can make the actors look as though they are overacting. As Downer points out, "a symbol can avoid calling attention to itself, and still perform its function."[20]

## The Emotional Context

We have discussed the use of film music as it assists in the characterization of people, both individually and collectively, and of ideas having symbolic implications. Music certainly works well when there is a need to bring out or enhance the emotional progression within a sequence. Some sequences have a basic feeling to them that remains unchanged throughout. These sequences generally call for a musical approach that focuses on the essential meaning and makes a comment. And there are times when the music is kept in reserve for the climactic peak of a scene, and the prevailing emotion is picked up on and extended by the music.

Other sequences consist of important shifts in feeling that necessitate shifts in the music. Finally, there are occasions that call for music that not only attends to the dramatic needs of the sequence in question, but takes a broad view having long-range implications for the entire film. In any instance, music can be a powerful aid in the attempt to shape and thus dramatize the emotional curve of a scene in ways that are consistent with the narrative line.

*Focus on the Essential Meaning*

Let us consider first a sequence in *The Children's Hour* (1962) in which music was needed to tie together various strands of meaning and make a comment.

In this sequence, which occurs near the beginning of the film, the opening six measures of the music pick up on the exuberance of the moment as Audrey Hepburn and James Garner drive off into the night. These measures, however, serve only as an introduction to an expansive melodic line (first stated in the main titles) that not only carries the rest of the scene but also touches upon the meaning of the sequence. The melodic line begins as the car disappears down the driveway followed by a cut to a long shot of the grounds in front of the schoolhouse. A few seconds later, there is a dissolve to Martha (Shirley MacLaine) as she walks down the driveway and pauses at the front gate. Nothing else happens—that is, there are no shifts in emotion that would require attention. The music reveals her state of mind.

The whole scene takes about forty seconds and is without dialogue. This can be a long time when little is happening on the screen, and it was Alex North's task to intensify the scene so that it would not appear overextended. Of greater importance was the significance of the scene and the way in which the music could bring that into focus. North found an answer that works on several levels. What had been a combination of problems— length, relatively little action without dialogue—became an opportunity.

The theme (beginning with measure 7) has a touching, lyrical quality that not only rebounds off the high spirits of the couple but also establishes a sense of well-being. This feeling is brought into association with the schoolhouse (now in the background of the shot) and, nine seconds later, is transferred to a sustained shot of MacLaine. A fundamental conflict within the story is brought out: While MacLaine seems slightly miffed by Garner's intrusion (MacLaine's cool reaction to Garner and her long walk amid the night shadows bring this out), she is nevertheless happy for Hepburn and their school's success.

In addition, the persuasive quality of the theme helps push forward the forty-second shot of MacLaine. Indeed, North needed forty seconds to make the musical comment. [*Divided into two phrases, the second phrase intensifies the scene by an ascending line and a tonicization of the lowered seventh degree (measures 15–18). As MacLaine stops at the gate, the music sustains the dominant of II, which is resolved in the next scene.*] In the context of the entire film, MacLaine's state of mind at this point is essential to the overall emotional curve of the story, for what follows (the loss of the school, public humiliation, and suicide) is anything but uplifting. (See Ex. II.17.)

*The Climactic Instant*

There are times when a long scene of contentious dialogue reaches a climax and the characters are left speechless; the camera holds on the shot, allowing the audience time to absorb the full impact of what has taken place. Music is called upon to accentuate this climactic instant as aftermath and to corroborate the prevailing emotions. An example of this occurs later on in

Ex. II.17.                    *The Children's Hour*

**Proposal**

Alex North

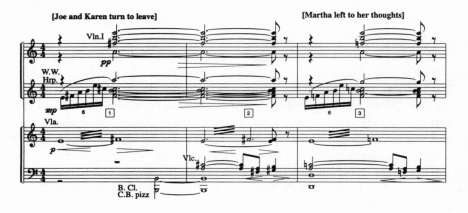

[Car pulls out of driveway.]

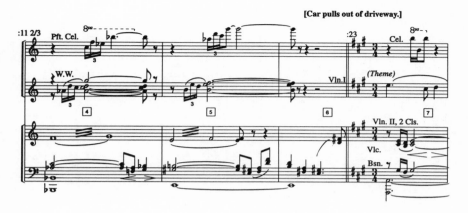

[l.s. of grounds in front of school house]

[Diss. to Martha walking plaintively in front of house]

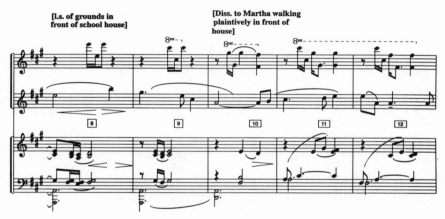

[Martha glances back at the house]

(continued)

*(continued)*

*The Children's Hour.* Rosalie, one of the students, has been coerced into confirming a lie that embroils the two teachers in alleged lesbianism. When the older woman in the film who has taken it upon herself to break the news to the parents is confronted by MacLaine and Hepburn, she asks Rosalie to repeat the story. Although Rosalie realizes that the teachers know she is lying, she feels she is in too deep and is afraid to tell the truth. In despair, she finally breaks down, sobbing. It becomes apparent, as the two teachers watch in mounting disbelief, that Rosalie is determined to stick to her story and that their case against her lie has been lost.

In the aftermath of this highly charged confrontation, North waits until the last possible moment before introducing music. First he builds upon Rosalie's sobbing, using five- and seven-note gestures in the bass. Each of these gestures is answered by dissonant-sounding chords, sustaining this moment of anguish. Initially, these chords are stated by the brass in straight mutes, the harsh sound corroborating the anger in the room. As the camera tightens on MacLaine, Hepburn, and Garner, the chords in measures 3–7 are given to the woodwinds. The softer sound of the woodwinds lends a sympathetic tone to the anguish experienced by the three principals. [*This feeling is deepened by the descending bass line as the F in measure 1 moves through E♭, D♭, C, and B♭ to the final A in measure 7.*] The accented moment and the jolting pace of the music produce a heart-stopping effect. (See Ex. II.18.)

Ex. II.18.                    *The Children's Hour*

## Confession

Alex North

*Shifts in Emotion*

The emotional curve of a scene can begin in innumerable ways, sometimes with a sustained moment of relative calm interrupted by an afterthought or sudden shift in emotion to another direction. In such cases, musical attention to detail is crucial. A pivotal scene in *Between Heaven and Hell,* a story that takes place during World War II, serves as an example of this. In this scene, Sam (Robert Wagner) attempts to recover, having just hurled grenades into a tunnel on the face of a cliff harboring an enemy gun nest. After he is pulled to safety, Sam collapses on the ground, and the music cue "Scared" is brought in.

Strings in two-part counterpoint carry the cue as Sam tries to catch his breath. When Sam lights a cigarette, composer Friedhofer introduces a sustained A♭ chord [*with an augmented fifth and a ninth*] that brings the sense of dramatic motion to a standstill. Suddenly, Sam shows signs of uncontrollable nervousness and begins to shake. Friedhofer accentuates the action with an E-minor triad [*with a seventh, ninth, and augmented eleventh*] superimposed over the A♭ chord for high strings and snare drum roll (played quietly), answered by piano and harp. The effect is subtle, and the moment is frozen to the spot. What might have passed as a minor event is given prominence by the music. This, in turn, prepares us for what is to come later on in the film as Sam's nervousness becomes an even larger issue. (See Ex. II.19.)

*Taking a Broad View*

On a large scale, involving the emotional curve and meaning of an entire film, music is sometimes needed at the end to pull things together into a single frame of reference. Naturally, composers would regard this as an essential part of the score. Generally, the music is taken from the previous cues and stated in a forthcoming manner. There are innumerable examples of this: *East of Eden, Who's Afraid of Virginia Woolf?, Laura, In Harm's Way, North by Northwest, Tom Horn,* and *Viva Zapata!* are just a few, all of which are discussed in this book. On occasion, preexisting concert pieces are used because of the tailor-made associations they evoke. In the best of situations they provide precisely what is needed. The music used for the conclusion of *Gallipoli* (1981) does just that. It offers a perspective on an extremely emotional situation, in which an entire company faces certain tragic death. This is what the film has been leading to all along. Regimental command has stubbornly ordered an open-field charge on the better-armed, entrenched enemy, knowing full well that few of their own, if any, will sur-

Ex. II.19.                   *Between Heaven and Hell*

## Scared

**Hugo Friedhofer**

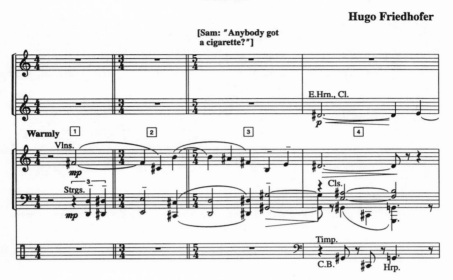

[Sam: "Anybody got a cigarette?"]

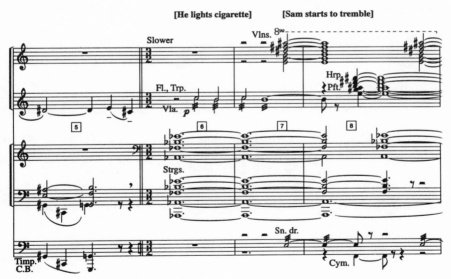

[He lights cigarette]        [Sam starts to tremble]

*(continued)*

*(continued)*

vive. Music is not needed to dramatize the action; the visual action takes care of the dramatic aspect. Music is used instead to comment on the emotionality of the moment within a broad context.

The Adagio in G Minor for Organ and Strings by Tomaso Albinoni, a Baroque opera composer, was chosen for this sequence. It was a splendid choice, providing a sense of sorrow, regret, and finality. The funereal plodding of the rhythm under a long legato melodic line was ideal, considering the impending outcome. The sound of the organ accentuated the religiousness of the moment, giving, as it were, last rites to the soldiers, a "supra reality" that you don't see on the screen. In all, the music becomes a hymn honoring these gallant men. It is revealing that the music, along with the implications of the story, is able to continue this train of thought through the end credits, after the film is over. Reference to a musical style from another century, and to this well-known work in particular, makes a statement that the meaning of what we have witnessed extends far beyond the story itself.

## Ambient Time and Place

Many films require music that is somehow associated with the time period or geographic location of the story. Some composers have elected to be as precise as possible in this regard. In his book *Soundtrack: The Music of the Movies,* Mark Evans reminds us that Miklos Rozsa drew heavily on the cantigas of twelfth-century Spain for his *El Cid* score (1951).[21] Less well known is that Bronislau Kaper obtained the help of ethnomusicologist Professor Mantle Hood to find Cambodian musical material and instruments to include in his score for *Lord Jim* (1965). An amusing and illustrative situation occurred when Leonard Rosenman went to South Dakota to find authentic musical material for *A Man Called Horse* (1970).

Rosenman sought out a group of men from the Sioux tribe in South Dakota's Black Hills. They graciously consented to sing various traditional songs, which he transcribed into musical notation. Suddenly, they stopped singing. Rosenman asked if there were more songs. Yes, they replied, but they were forbidden to sing them to anyone but a verifiable medicine man. After an awkward silence, one of the men asked Rosenman what he was writing. He explained that composers are trained to write down music by ear. The group was so impressed that they decided to make Rosenman a medicine man right there and then. After his investiture, the tribesmen sang him the rest of their songs. I will never know if these latter songs were actually used in Rosenman's score. He refuses to tell me unless I become similarly appointed.

Music identified with cultural, ethnic, or national origins plays a decisive role in the characterization of time and place in film, and examples of such use abound. Alex North's music for *Viva Zapata!* (1952) evokes traditional Mexican culture so convincingly that the essence of key scenes, as they are accompanied by music, becomes firmly rooted in the driving spirit of that culture. Jerry Goldsmith's score for *The Boys from Brazil* opens with such a characteristically full-blown Viennese-style waltz that it would be impossible to associate it with any place other than Vienna (where Laurence Olivier's character resides). The accompaniment to the waltz as well as fragments from the melodic line serves as a link to the percussive music for other scenes in Paraguay. *On the Beach* takes place primarily in Australia, and producer Stanley Kramer insisted that Ernest Gold use "Waltzing Matilda" as his primary material. Gold, at first reluctant to do so, explains that he soon found that the song worked well and was adaptable to almost endless variation. Gold's reference to the theme provides some of the most poignant characterization within the film.

In the above illustrations, the music serves as an associative element that is identified with a particular place or environment. But establishing the time or era in which a story takes place is another matter altogether. Chronological time, as it relates to musical style, is not so easy to pin down. For example, only a highly sophisticated listener or a well-schooled musician or musicologist could differentiate between European music of the 1450s and that of half a century later. There are overlapping stylistic currents as well. Bach, for instance, is generally considered the epitome of the Baroque, and yet his music was actually conservative for its time; many of his contemporaries were on the brink of the classical style of early Haydn. This tendency toward stylistic overlapping is true of virtually every period of music history, especially in the twentieth century.

Precision regarding historical era and musical style is not always that critical. The dramatic needs of the story can be met as well, if not more effectively, by association involving a more generalized concept as by historical documentation. For example, there have been many films about the life and times of Jesus. Even if Western music from that specific time had been preserved in written form (and to my knowledge, none has), we must wonder if it would match the sweeping grandeur and significance of that moment in history, particularly as it is presented on the large screen. Instead, many film scores have successfully captured the impact and spirituality of that era through reference to more recent musical styles and techniques. David Raksin's score for *The Redeemer* (1966) employs a style associated with the Baroque period, especially as is found in Bach's masses, combined with certain twentieth-century practices. The connection is clear. Hugo Friedhofer cited the *Redeemer* score as the best ever written for a subject of this kind. Alfred Newman's score for *The Robe* (1953) takes a much different tack. He relies upon the tonal idiom of Richard Strauss, and, in addi-

tion, many cues are stylistically reminiscent of Rimsky-Korsakov and De-
bussy.

Films depicting contemporary times present more exacting problems and
challenges, for we are more sensitive to the changing musical styles of our
own period, especially as they relate to our personal experiences. On at
least one level, the problem of establishing a current time frame can be
solved with music derived from popular idioms generally associated with a
particular decade. The music for *Raging Bull* (1980), the story about the
1940s prizefighter Jake LaMotta, consists almost entirely of swing-band ar-
rangements of standard tunes identified with that era. *Al Capone,* which
takes place in Chicago, includes an extension of 1920s jazz in its main titles
music and other scenes.

Reference to popular music idioms leads to what is known in the industry as "source music." This subject is sufficiently interesting and complex to
warrant special consideration within the larger context of characterization.
Before doing this, however, I wish to make one additional comment about
music that relates to the time period of a story. I know that many directors
are insistent upon having music that is immediately associated with the
period in which the story takes place. Some have been exacting about this,
perhaps too much so. One director said, "This film takes place in 1902,"
and he asked the composer to "write in the style that was popular in that
year." He may just as well have stipulated spring or early fall. It is always
tempting to place a high priority on the connection between time period
and music. It is, after all, a viable, naturalistic approach. And it has proven
to be extremely effective, and often necessary in many cases. But it is not
the only approach, by a long shot. If the time of the story is obvious and not
needful of musical corroboration, a different musical style not necessarily
associated with the period might better serve the needs of the picture.
Goldsmith's score for *Chinatown* (1978) was not written in the popular style
of the early 1930s but in a much more personal dramatic style that identified with a far wider range of dramatic needs. Most composers take this
possibility into consideration. In my opinion, a mindless insistence on music that relates only to the period of the story while ignoring other needs
has limited if not disturbing consequences.

## Source Music

Source music is introduced into a scene either visually or by reference. We
see a dance band playing in a dance hall, or we see (and hear) a radio or
television. If a person is playing an instrument, singing, or whistling, we

see and hear the performer. These sounds are visually initiated. In other instances, the source of sound is not shown on screen. At an ice rink, the organist (or, in today's culture, a disco system) may not be seen, but we can expect to hear one. Or reference might be made to the boy next door who is practicing on his clarinet or to the louts upstairs who are playing heavy metal music at 100 decibels. "Muzak" is, of course, all too commonplace in hotel lobbies, elevators, shopping malls, and airline terminals. These sounds are characteristic of those environments and have a life of their own. By association, these sounds can offer a comment on a scene, and as such they present an opportunity for the composer.

A restaurant scene from *Giant* (1956) is a case in point. Here, the exact choice of source music makes a statement that goes to the essence of the entire scene. In this scene, Rock Hudson and his family enter a roadside restaurant and the camera zooms in on the jukebox, which is playing an upbeat, jingoistic version of "The Yellow Rose of Texas," sung by a glee club. The proprietor objects to the presence of Hudson's Mexican daughter-in-law and grandson and makes a racial slur. At this point, the music ends. Later, another Mexican family enters, and the owner orders them to leave. Hudson, having reached the limits of his tolerance, gets into a fight with the proprietor. The source music is brought back into the scene and, because of its character and content, makes the proprietor's position all the more mindless. The tune itself—and the carefree way it is sung—is an excellent choice for the situation. Original "dramatic" music might have lent credence to the proprietor's attitude by making him appear more important than he really is.

A hilarious use of source music is found in Mel Brooks's *Blazing Saddles* (1974). Like all true comedic geniuses, Brooks forces us to reexamine convention and to see the commonplace from a different angle. In one scene, we see the newly appointed sheriff (Cleavon Little) riding across the desert decked out in a gold suede outfit with Western fringing. His horse matches the color of his outfit, and his saddlebags are ostentatiously branded with the Gucci trademark. In the background, we hear a sophisticated swing-band arrangement of "April in Paris." Suddenly the Count Basie Orchestra (wearing tuxedos) comes into full view. The sheriff smiles and waves at the Count, and the nineteenth-century desert becomes a swinging place.

### Integrating Source Music with Original Music

Source music is often integrated with the original or dramatic score, and with effective results. This has been accomplished in several ways. One way is to rework principal thematic material for use as source music. This is like looking at another side of a character in a plot, although in this case we are speaking of a musical character. In a scene from *The Misfits* (1974), Eli Wallach turns on the radio and invites Marilyn Monroe to dance. The source music on the radio is a dance-band arrangement of the main titles theme.

Initially, the music used for the main titles was marked "Broad, expressive" (measure 5) and set for orchestra. (See Ex. II.20.)

Ex. II.20.                    *The Misfits*

### Main Titles

The dance-band arrangement totally recasts the nature and style of the theme. One interesting aspect is how the source music leads into what happens in the next scene. Monroe (Roslyn) steps outside the house and, in an ethereal manner, continues to dance alone in the garden among the trees. She has momentarily retreated into her own world, and Alex North, dropping the dance-band style, eases into an elaborate variation of the theme for full orchestra. In this way, North brings the two scenes into close correspondence and underlines the shift in meaning of the shot in the garden. (See Ex. II.21.)

Ex. II.21.                              *The Misfits*

# Roslyn

**Alex North**

Another way of integrating source music with original music is to dove-tail or overlap dramatic material with source music in much the same way as an editor makes a slow dissolve between two different images. This over-lapping technique—in which the end of one kind of music overlaps with the beginning of another kind of music (as in music by Charles Ives)—not only provides musical continuity but also leads to effective musical and dramatic results.

There are, however, times when independent source material exists like an island, unchallenged by the dramatic score or isolated from it. The po-tential, and need, for integration is often minimized in such a case. Yet subtle connections can be made. In Robert Altman's *Fool for Love* (1985), I was faced with a situation in which the first fifteen minutes of the film (including main titles) called almost entirely for country and western tunes that, for the most part, functioned as source music. The tunes were written by playwright and star Sam Shepard's sister, Sandy Rogers. Altman and I decided to introduce orchestral dramatic music at a point in the film when the story shifted gears, because we wanted to deepen the emotional effect and make a musical comment on the nature and meaning of the shift. We both felt this would be difficult, if not impossible, to accomplish with a country and western tune. The problem was finding an orchestral sound and contrapuntal texture that would somehow deliver the dramatic goods and still connect with the source music. I agonized over this problem be-cause of the simplistic nature of the tunes, and finally decided to use the opening four notes of the main titles song, treating them as a four-note cell and as a basis for variation for the first orchestral cue. (See Ex. II.22a, b.) Additionally, I chose a harmonic texture that consisted mainly of fourth

Ex. II.22a.                          *Fool for Love*

**Sandy Rogers**

Come    on    ba - by    let's    ride

Ex. II.22b.

chords, so as to produce an open sound. These factors allowed for a sense of coexistence between source and dramatic music. (See Ex. II.23.)

When source music is well chosen, it can be the best possible means of fulfilling an environmental expectation or need and thus be of value in the characterization process. Integrating source music with original dramatic music is not always a necessity; in many cases, the source music stands on its own. When, for example, the starchy, white-dressed naval officers attend a dance at the Pearl Harbor Officers' Club in *In Harm's Way* (1965), Jerry Goldsmith's arrangement of an original tune fits the time, place, and circumstances. It was not necessary for him to derive that tune from other portions of the score. In fact, it may even have proved confusing had he done so.

Ex. II.23.                              *Fool for Love*

## "So What?"

George Burt

*(continued)*

*(continued)*

*Chapter Three*

# Emphasizing the Dramatic Line

David Raksin tells about a sequence he scored several years ago in which gradual shifts in pacing on the screen provided him with an intriguing opportunity. It was a Western film in which one of the characters (Reginald Gardiner), who had been running with a gang of desperados, wanted to quit and lead another life, but the gang felt he knew too much. Raksin:

Later, he is alone, walking along a street, and he keeps looking over his shoulder. After a while, he becomes conscious of someone following him. He walks faster and faster and, finally, he breaks into a run. He leaps under a wagon, and the other guy catches up with him and kills him. Ordinarily, in those days, the music accelerated as the action sped up. What I did was this: As the fellow walked faster I kept the music going at the same dragging tempo. It was like stretching a rubber band, and when I finally let it go, it snapped. The instant the music took off there was such a disparity in the new tempo that, in a way, the moment was overdramatized. But it was terrific. If you were in the audience and you weren't listening consciously to the music, you would feel something was dragging, as though something was holding him back. You wouldn't know what it was, but it would make you say, "For God's sake, man, start running!"[1]

This is an excellent example of what music can contribute in the way of pacing. In this case, the cue was intended to bring us to the edge of our seats, and by holding off until the last possible instant before changing tempo, it also provided a decisive accent to a strategic point in the scene. Through this sudden change you knew all hell was soon to break loose.

The marriage between music and film, both temporal art forms, demands that inherent aspects of accent (and pacing) in each medium are brought into correspondence within a dramatic context. In this chapter, I will point out several examples that underline this kinetic function of music in film.

## Musical Accents

Accenting something is one of the most important functions of film music. Mark Evans recalls that in the silent days, "a pianist might, for example, be advised to break a piece of pottery in order to frighten the audience when they saw the phantom!"[2] To be sure, the use of musical accent has become infinitely more subtle and complex since that time.

### Music Entrances

Composers have to be careful about how and when they introduce music to a scene, because a sudden entrance in and of itself can constitute an accent. Accents attract attention and thus can raise questions about something happening on the screen. For instance, imagine a sequence that opens with a man checking into a hotel. He takes his luggage to the room and then goes to the hotel dining room. We know he is a major character, or at least someone to whom we should pay attention, because the camera has singled him out. But let us assume that music has been omitted in the sequence so far. Then the camera cuts to a woman who is checking into the same hotel, and music is suddenly brought in. The music entrance would raise a question not only about the woman but also, possibly, about her relationship to the man as well: Is she his ex-wife, lover, creditor? If such questions are integral to the plot, then the music entrance performs a real function as accent.

Composers often express a concern about being too obvious with a music entrance. They worry that if it is too sudden it will call attention to itself and thus be a distraction to the story. To this, Raksin comments,

> We all tend to be too self-conscious about bringing in music. We don't realize that if the audience is with us, they're going to accept it. But let's say that there is a place where you need a musical accent and you don't want to wait until then to introduce the music. One solution is to precede this point with music written in what used to be called a neutral style—a word I always despised, but now I see its use—and you will be there to make the accent.[3]

The entry point for music is always a concern. And it is best when this point has a dramatic function. Ernest Gold expresses a thought shared by many film composers:

When I first started in the business, the old school of thought was that you go for the physical thing—somebody closing a door, somebody hanging up the phone, that sort of thing. I prefer to find a meaning or a change in the dramatic line to justify a musical entrance. This might be triggered by what somebody says or by a look in someone's face. Something that justifies dramatically, not mechanically. The other method, which is action-oriented without meaning, I hate. That's the faucet form of movie scoring—you turn it on and you turn it off.[4]

Scenes invariably begin with a film cut. Editors have the choice of making a hard (sudden) cut or a soft cut with a fade-in characteristic. There is also the possibility of a dissolve, in which, for a fraction of a second, the new scene is superimposed on the previous one. Whatever the choice, the problem arises when the new scene requires a music entrance. Gold says he has always hated to start music on a cut, because it draws so much attention to the visual change. One way around this, he points out, is "to begin with an upbeat or a pick-up gesture in the music, not a downbeat, to counteract the fact that the music starts with the change."[5]

*Reaction and Cutaway Shots*

Film, unlike theater, is uniquely capable of cutting from one person to another. This can involve a reaction shot. A music entrance on the cut to a reaction will emphasize the way in which something is coming across more than what is actually being said or done. However, situations involving several cuts accompanied by continuous music create a special problem, particularly if the music is needed to emphasize various changes of tone or meaning underlying each reaction. Gold has mentioned that "the obvious thing to do is to bring in muted brass or something like that for an accent, even if it's very soft. But there are other ways that are much more subtle." He describes how, in some instances, he has written a short fugato and timed it so that the "next voice, without any noticeable accent, comes in on the cut. The fact that there is a musical event at all is enough to make the point."[6]

Regarding cutaway shots, Gold says he had a difficult problem in *It's a Mad, Mad, Mad, Mad World* (1963).

You had all these different strands, people going in different directions, and you had to cut from one to the other. If the music followed everyone—twenty seconds of this, fifteen seconds of that—it would emphasize the choppiness of the film, and after a while the audience

would cry for mercy. What to do? I hit upon the device of a continuing element in the music, a melodic line, and changed the accompaniment on the cuts to go with what was actually seen on the screen.
The changes involved different textures, sounds, and ranges. In this
way, I was able to keep the overall view, musically speaking, and at
the same time put the spotlight on various people. This was consciously done. It was a necessity.[7]

*The Element of Surprise*

In many films, the element of surprise is a key issue. Take a mystery involving a courtroom setting in which one of the witnesses turns out to be the
murderer at the end. Since musical punctuation of his appearances could
give everything away, it is standard practice to point the finger of suspicion
at someone else to allow for the unexpected. However, in very complicated
mysteries, this approach becomes extremely complex. In *Sleuth* the burden
of guilt switches from one person to another and back again in rapid succession. John Addison's score was both theatrical and light in character, and
because of this he was able to set up each situation in such a way that a
retraction of sorts was always possible.

In horror films, musical accent takes on special uses. Aside from the
obvious, which primarily includes backing up a horrendous action with a
hair-raising musical gesture, composers have tried different ways of approaching a situation. Rosenman recalls a film he did with John Franken-
heimer. It wasn't a great film, Rosenman says, but it was fun to do.

It was a monster movie, and there was a long sequence in which these
people are riding in a jeep at night. The camera pans into the bushes
now and then, and we're all scared to death because we expect the
monster to jump out at any time. I said to John, "Let's try something.
Let me throw in some red herrings, a couple of dissonant chords, and
scare the hell out of the audience, because, after all, the function of a
monster movie is to scare everybody. The audience will be relieved
and say the monster is not there. Then, when it appears, that will
really scare them." John said, "Okay, let's try it." Later, at the previews
in Texas, people jumped up and screamed when those chords came
in. It was terrific, but then one reviewer complained that the music
came in at the wrong place![8]

Composers have many ways of achieving an accent. A sustained chord,
the beginning of a contrasting melodic line, and a resolution to a new tonal

area are all viable means of pointing up an event. A resolution or cadence to a new or old tonal region produces what Roger Sessions called an accent of weight. There are, of course, many other possibilities. The high point of the line, for instance, generates a climactic effect. In some cases, this may be true of the low point as well. A change in the orchestration or a change in texture (such as a shift from a chordal texture to one that is more polyphonic in nature) produces an accent of sorts. Certainly the many aspects of rhythm—including the rate of change in harmonic rhythm—exist as endless resources in this regard.

## Plateaus of Thought

There are times when subtle shifts to plateaus of thought in a dialogue require equally subtle accents in the music. This is a frequent problem in film composing, and good solutions demand an extremely perceptive understanding of underlying meanings as compared with what is actually being said.

In a moving scene in *Separate Tables* (1958), music enters at a crucial turning point during an extended dialogue between two of the leading characters. The manner in which it is brought in and the material chosen for the opening of the cue delicately respond to an excruciating moment of truth prompted by a recent disclosure about one of the characters. More important is how the music, in conjunction with the dialogue, evolves into a progression along several subtly implied plateaus of thought.

Scored by David Raksin with a screenplay by Terence Rattigan, the film takes place in a small seaside hotel in Bournemouth, England. The scene in question involves David Niven as the major and Deborah Kerr as Sybil, a spinster who is pathetically dominated by her suspicious mother (Gladys Cooper). The mother has discovered that the major had recently been arrested for accosting a girl at the cinema, and to make matters worse, she has also learned that he was not a major who had distinguished himself in battle, as he had told everyone, but rather a lieutenant who had served in a relatively unimportant capacity on the home front. Sybil, the spinster, has admired the major in a quiet, repressed way and, being vulnerable and inexperienced, has been taken in by his charm. She is devastated when she learns of his indiscretions. In the scene entitled "A Step Further," the major joins Sybil on the terrace, where she confronts him with his lies. He attempts to explain, but the explanations are too anguishing for her. Sobbing, she says, "Stop it. I don't want to hear any more." In answer to this, the major confides, "I wanted to talk to somebody about it. I never have, you see, not in my whole life." There is a slight pause and the music enters, with a held F♯ in the bassoon followed by a fragment of the theme that has become associated with Niven's character.

When discussing the character of the major, Raksin says, "Niven was so wonderful in that role, it broke my heart. And there was something so vulnerable about the character who had to pretend to be a high-ranking officer, having fought battles and all that, and who could only approach sex in the dark, that I felt I needed something that would combine these elements. Somehow, an old Scottish tune occurred to me called 'Wha Wadna Fecht fer Charlie' (Who Wouldn't Fight for Charlie), and it seemed right for the character."[9] Raksin opens the cue with a fragment of this theme in a subdued but jaunty manner for the bassoon.

During the statement of the theme (in the key of F♯), the major apologizes to Sybil for upsetting her "of all people." Sybil asks, "Why me, especially?" and the major answers that he doesn't "give a hang about the others." On this line the music settles on a B-minor chord, bringing the fragment of the tune to an end and allowing for a pause so that the implications of his words may be weighed. (See Ex. III.1, measures 1–3.) What follows is a short transitional passage during which the major assumes that the revelations about him won't mean much to the others, but "it will be different for you, Sybil, and that makes me very unhappy." (See Ex. III.1, measures 4–6.) The music again pauses on the last few words, as though to take a breath, and then moves to a complex sonority constructed with the superimposition of G-minor and E♭-major triads.

[*The motion within this transitional passage is made even more apparent by the ascending, continuous eighth-note movement and the highly chromatic content throughout. This contrasts with the diatonic nature of the opening tune. However, the arrival point on the superimposed triads (measure 6) is sustained for two measures, which exist as another plateau in the music. This new level corresponds with the subsequent change of direction in the dialogue.*] Sybil slowly turns to the major and says, "That's the first time you called me Sybil." The major, feeling even more awkward at this point, asks, "Is it really?" and, trying to be brave, he looks away and says, "Uh . . . there's not much point in that . . . stuff now." On the word "now," Raksin brings back the ascending subsidiary four-note idea that was introduced in the transitional passage and which, by the way, is derived from the first measure of the major's theme. [*This appears now in quarter-note values (i.e., in augmentation) for cello at the end of measure 8, and it functions as an upbeat to another shift in the direction of the dialogue.*]

Sybil then asks in a desperate tone, "What makes me so different from the others?" Here, the focus of the scene shifts from the major to Sybil. Responding to her feeling of urgency, Raksin increases the tempo slightly

Ex. III.1.                          *Separate Tables*

## A Step Further

**David Raksin**

*(continued)*

and states the ascending four-note motive once again, this time in the oboe d'amore part (see measure 9). [*Harmonically, this brings the passage to a momentary rest on A♭ as Sybil's theme (introduced in the opening of the film) now reappears in the oboe part (see measures 10–12).*] The major hesitates and then attempts an answer: "I suppose it's because you're so scared of . . . well, shall we call it life? It sounds more respectable than that word I know you hate [that is, sex]." A

*(continued)*

pause on the A♭ harmony along with the questioning nature of Sybil's theme allows for hesitation before the answer. It is a complex beginning of a cue involving several plateaus of thought within a short period of time. It continues beyond what has been discussed here and is well worth further study.

### Accent by Omission

The end of a musical cue forms an accent of a special kind—an accent by omission. Occasionally, the music can end with a bang, especially if it leads up to an action (such as someone entering a room), or with an abrupt cutoff to prepare for a shot requiring absolute silence. Or it can end in a quiet way, where its absence is barely noticeable.

Consider a sequence in which the camera follows someone walking along the street. There is no dialogue; the person is in deep thought about where he is going and what he is going to say when he gets there. Situations of this kind frequently arise in film. Assume that the shot calls for music to underline or characterize the nature of his thinking and that music is not needed once the dialogue begins. When can the music be taken out? One possibility is to end it a fraction of a second before the first line. This approach tends to emphasize the opening statement. A smoother way of leading into the dialogue is to hold the music through the first few words. This connects what has transpired with the next shot, allowing the music to "bleed" into the new situation. It can be accomplished in different ways: by sustaining a chord in the strings or winds, or by writing the last sound for an instrument such as the vibraphone, harp, or piano and letting the sound die out on its own.  If more emphasis is needed, the ending might involve a change of register, where the music is transferred from the low strings and finished in the flute or piccolo.

Composers also point out that sometimes it seems virtually impossible to find an appropriate place to bring the music to an end. For instance, in *Mad World,* Gold describes an extended chase that required music, but "there was a scene toward the end of the chase where music would have been absolutely wrong, and I had no place to go out. So as the chase goes on, I wrote it so that the whole orchestral texture jells into percussive chords with ever-lengthening pauses, and after a longer pause, it never comes back."[10]

## The Missing Beat or Pulse

On occasion a sequence will have the appearance of unwittingly falling apart or becoming too erratic. This may be the fault of the editing, in which case there is little a composer can do about it. But when the dramatic nature and intent of the sequence necessarily leans in that direction and the editor wants to push it as far as possible for effect, the composer might be asked if there is something the music can do that will in some way hold things together and still not cancel out the desired effect.

Consider the opening of *Tom Jones* (1963), for instance. There is no ambient sound. The actions take place on a seventeenth-century English estate, and the story begins with the news that one of the maids has given birth to an illegitimate child—Tom Jones. Certain people are scandalized by this turn of events, and the screen action is frenetic. The music by John Addison is written in the style of an improvisational silent movie piano with a Baroque influence, where the feeling of a steady beat is common practice. This steady beat is in direct contrast to the jerky cuts in the sequence; it provides a rhythmic frame of reference. Thus the beat or musical pulse plays a decisive role in bringing things together. It makes the jumpy quality of the film more acceptable, and as an added plus, the effect is totally congruent with the comedic intent of the sequence.

### An Actor's Inner Rhythm

It is said that actors respond, in part, to a kind of inner rhythm when playing a role. If so, it is probably unconscious. However, Philip Baker

Hall, one of the most accomplished actors I have known, said he had various tempi or beats deliberately in mind when he delivered the ninety-minute monologue in *Secret Honor*. Hall's comment carries weight, since *Secret Honor* is a one-character, one-set film, and his demanding role moves between extreme emotional highs and lows for extended periods of time. His extraordinary performance, in combination with Robert Altman's direction and use of the camera, is absolutely compelling from beginning to end.[11] Before I attempted to compose the music for *Secret Honor*, I remember listening to the dialogue over and over again while watching Hall's every move. I wanted to arrive at something that would juxtapose neatly with the rhythmic flow of Hall's performance and still not get in the way. At certain points I was able to discern an inner sense of timing. Later, after the score was written, Hall told me about his technique of having a separate tempo or pulse for each scene. He said this gave him a sense of flow and continuity.

Several years ago, I bought a print of Charlie Chaplin's *The Rink* (1917) for an experiment using different kinds of music. One scene in particular caused me to wonder about the rhythmic aspect of his acting and the special implications it might have for music. In this fast-moving scene, Chaplin mixes the ingredients for a cocktail, and he adds anything within easy grasp: scotch, gin, eggs, flowers, and so on. After repeated viewings, I realized Chaplin was responding to some kind of rhythmic pulse or beat. Once I found the tempo and played music in that same tempo along with the film, the scene suddenly took on a special vitality. Chaplin's quick actions were sometimes in syncopation with the beat, and at important points within the scene they were right *on* the beat. The music supplied the missing pulse, and the effect was even more comical than before. I don't know whether Chaplin consciously worked with a pulse in mind, but his consistency was amazing. One explanation is that many silent films were shot with a small ensemble of off-camera musicians simultaneously playing music appropriate to the scene to help establish the mood for the actors. Possibly, a musical pulse was a factor in how the scenes were acted out.

*Supra Rhythmic Structure*

Many scenes have depended on the compelling effect of a steady beat or musical pulse to sustain a needed momentum over a long span of time. A striking instance of this appears in a sequence at the end of *Between Heaven and Hell*. The music, and the way it works with the sequence, is worth studying. It not only illustrates the effectiveness of a steady beat; it takes this issue one step further by showing that a given musical form can provide a supra rhythmic structure on a broad scale. To do this, Hugo Friedhofer composed a four-part fugue exposition followed by several subject entries in another key. The fugue climaxes strategically with two statements of the "Dies Irae" (Day of Wrath). Among other things, the evenly placed subject entries, together with an effect of accumulating intensity indigenous to the fugue form, create the large-scale rhythmic pulse mentioned above. The result is nothing less than a tour de force.

In this sequence, Sam (Robert Wagner) races down a mountainside to get help for his wounded buddy. It is a long sequence without dialogue, and our attention is focused solely upon Sam's desperate attempt to maneuver through Japanese troops as he runs at top speed. The sheer urgency of his race is instantly heightened at the outset by a two-measure ostinato figure for percussion that is maintained for the length of the cue. However, it is not the percussion alone that makes the point. The rhythmic feel of the fugue structure itself begins to have an enormous impact, and this is extended all the way to the end of the sequence. (See Ex. III.2.)

The way in which this formal music design fits the action is extraordinary. [*The fugue subject appears at the instant Sam begins to run (measure 3). It is stated by timpani and piano and punctuated by growling trombones, which add a dramatically rough-hewn sense of determination to the scene. The answer to the subject, stated by clarinets, violas, and horns in measure 14, concurs with a cut to a rear-angle shot of Sam. Strings and bassoons provide the countersubject. The third statement of the fugue subject, measure 24, corresponds to a close-up of Sam's blurred feet. Toward the middle of this third statement, measure 30, Friedhofer introduces a woodwind doubling at the octave to further dramatize Sam's encounter with the Japanese soldiers as he hits them with the butt of his rifle. The fourth subject statement, given to trombones and tuba in the low register, arrives just a single second before a cut to other Japanese soldiers down the trail. (See measure 35.)*]

[*The beginning of the first episode coincides with a shot of a Japanese soldier who has paused on the trail to study a map (measure 46). This episode functions tonally as a transition to a new harmonic area representing the second stage of the fugue. As Sam runs past the soldiers, they turn in chase. This then begins the second stage of the sequence. At this instant, the horns (ff) are given the subject in a new key (measure 52). The second episode connects with an additional cutaway shot to the soldiers, now in hot pursuit (measure 81).*]

At a crucial moment, Sam trips and scrambles to pick up his rifle. It is obvious that the enemy is bearing down on him. Friedhofer intensifies this moment with another statement of the fugue subject for horns (measure 87), later doubled by trumpets at the octave. The shooting begins and Sam is hit. This marks the end of the fugue, which in this instance may have existed as an analogue to the chase, at least in spirit, and the first statement of the "Dies Irae" is brought in at this point (measure 108). Sam manages to elude capture

Ex. III.2.                    *Between Heaven and Hell*

# Desperate Journey

Hugo Friedhofer

*(continued)*

*(continued)*

(continued)

*(continued)*

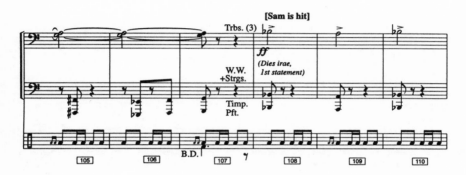

*(continued)*

*(continued)*

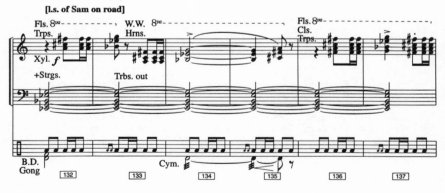

(continued)

*(continued)*

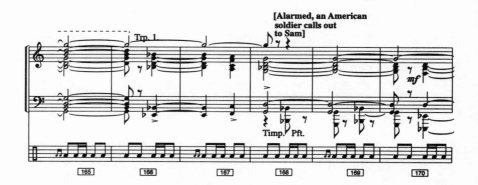

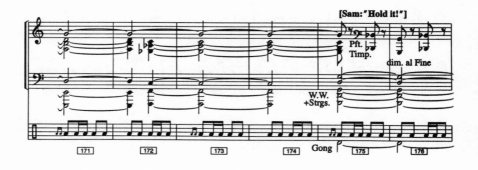

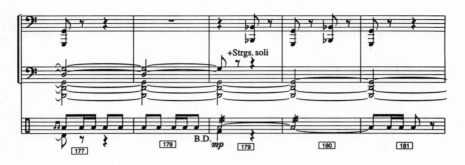

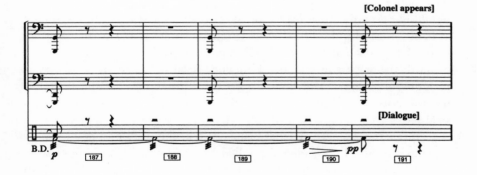

and continues down the hill until he reaches his base of operations. The sheer momentum of the music throughout and the steady beat gradually disappear. The cue ends as the colonel appears and asks for a report.

As the formal scheme of this cue adheres to the cutting of the film in such a remarkable way, it would seem that Friedhofer had at least some say in the editing process. But Richard Fleischer, the director of the film, states that this was not the case. In tribute to Fleischer's dramatic talent, the scene initially was cut in a way that made formal sense. And it was Friedhofer's creative insight that brought the fugue structure into correspondence with that formal shape. Most important, the result creates a dramatic explosiveness that was needed at this climactic point in the film.

*Coalescence of Images*

There is, of course, a difference between how we perceive a play in the theater and its dramatization on film. This perceptual difference explains why a play works perfectly well without music, whereas the same play adapted for the screen requires music. One would think that because of all the cinematographic techniques available—change of camera angle, close-ups, and various other kinds of shots—that it would be the other way around: that plays would require music and that film would be self-sufficient. As many writers have already expressed their views on this complex matter, even a cursory summation of their views is unnecessary. But I would like to point to at least one aspect that has a bearing on the subject at hand: musical pulse. To do this I suggest we look at a particular scene from *Who's Afraid of Virginia Woolf?*, since the play had enormous success on both the stage and screen. The scene itself is so moving it is easy to imagine an audience not taking a breath throughout. Yet the matter of musical pulse is a factor in the way this scene is perceived on film, as we shall see.

In this scene, George (Richard Burton) tells the story of a boy he knew in prep school who accidentally killed his mother with a shotgun some years before. One evening, several of the boys went to a gin mill to "drink with the grown-ups and listen to the jazz." The young boy who had killed his mother ordered "bergin and water." His innocence evoked ripples of laughter. George goes on to tell what happened to the boy in later years and describes how another accident resulted in his father's death.

Burton's story can be summed up in a few sentences. Yet the cue goes on for about four minutes, and the effect is spellbinding. Why? The script is pure theater with a built-in concession to drunken, repetitive, snail's-pace recitation. More important is the tragic story itself. In the theater, this monologue plays extremely well without music because of the distance between actor and audience in a live performance. An aura of collective involvement in what is being said spreads throughout the audience. But the situation is different in a movie theater. Close-ups of Burton projected on a large screen make every detail of his facial expressions apparent. This acts upon our senses and we begin to participate in a variety of ways, creating our own images and notions of continuity. The need for music here originates, in part, with the necessity for a coalescence of these images into a directed pattern. A rhythmic frame of reference or sense of pulse can contribute to this process.

The timing sheet for this scene shows many things, including the complete monologue, subtle camera movements, and cutting. Notice that the pauses, no matter how slight, are boxed in the left-hand column to represent the timings. The abbreviation for "over the shoulder" is o.s. Words describing camera motion and type of shot are capitalized. Pauses are also in caps. This method is effective when scanning the timing sheet. (See Ex. III.3.)

Ex. III.3.          *Who's Afraid of Virginia Woolf?*

Reel 6, Part I: Cue Sheet

| Timing | Action | Footage |
|---|---|---|
| | George, seated and leaning against large tree, begins Bergin story. George: "And he had killed his mother with a shotgun some years before." | |
| :00 | PAUSE. MED. CLOSE-UP. GEORGE as he looks down toward ground. CAMERA very slowly MOVES IN. | 0' |
| :01 | George raises his head slightly and looks o.s. as he continues: "Accidentally, completely accidentally, without an unconscious motivation, I have no doubt, no doubt at all." | 1' 8" |
| :07 1/3 | PAUSE. "What's more," George reflects and looks down toward ground— | 11' |
| :08 1/3 | "and this one time, this boy went with us. And we ordered our drinks and when it came his turn, he said—" | 12' 8" |
| :16 2/3 | PAUSE. CAMERA CONTINUES its SLOW MOVE IN— | 25' |

| Timing | Action | Footage |
|---|---|---|
| :18 | George continues: "I'll have Bergin. Give me some Bergin, please." | 27' |
| :23 1/3 | PAUSE. George looks o.s. toward Nick. George (looks o.s. toward Nick): "Bergin and water." | 35' |
| :25 1/3 | PAUSE. | 38' |
| :28 | George looks once more straight ahead as he reflects. George: "Well, we all laughed—He was blond and he had the face of a cherub and we all laughed." | 42' |
| :36 | PAUSE. CAMERA VERY CLOSE to George as it continues its very SLOW MOVE IN. | 54' |
| :36 2/3 | George: "And his cheeks went red and the color rose in his neck. The waiter told the people at the next table what he had said, and then they laughed and more people were told and the laughter grew and more people and more laughed." | 55' |
| :51 1/3 | PAUSE. END OF CAMERA MOVEMENT. CLOSE SHOT of George as he continues to look down toward ground. | 77' |
| :53 | George sighs: "And a—" | 79' 8" |
| :54 | PAUSE—Deep emotion— | 81' 8" |
| :56 | George: "No one was laughing more than us, and none of us more than the boy who had shot his mother." | 84' |
| 1:03 1/3 | PAUSE. | 95' |
| 1:05 1/3 | George continues: "And soon, everyone in the gin mill knew what the laughter was about and everyone started ordering Bergin—" | 98' |
| 1:12 1/3 | PAUSE. George glances o.s. toward Nick: "and laughed when they ordered it." | 108' 8" |
| 1:14 2/3 | PAUSE, once more. George looks forward down toward ground. George: "And soon, of course, the laughter became less general but it did not subside—" | 112' |
| 1:20 1/3 | PAUSE. | 120' 9" |

| Timing | Action | Footage |
|---|---|---|
| 1:21 2/3 | George: "entirely for a very long time. For always at this table or that someone would order Bergin." | 122' 5" |
| 1:29 | George, again, says— | 133' 8" |
| 1:30 1/3 | George: "and a whole new area of laughter would rise." | 135' 8" |
| 1:33 2/3 | PAUSE. | 142' 9" |
| 1:36 | George (continuing): "We drank free that night and we were bought champagne by management—" | 144' |
| 1:41 1/3 | PAUSE. George (quickly glances once more toward Nick): "by the gangster father of one of us." | 152' |
| 1:44 2/3 | PAUSE. George turns forward again. | 157' |
| 1:46 2/3 | George: "And of course we suffered—the next day, each of us, alone, on his train away from the city and each of us with ah—" | 160' |
| 1:57 2/3 | PAUSE. As he continues to remember back. | 176' 9" |
| 1:59 | George: "grown-up's hangover. But it was the grandest day—of my—" | 178' 10" |
| 2:07 1/3 | PAUSE. George raises his head slightly— | 191' |
| 2:09 1/3 | George (softly): "youth." | 194' |
| 2:11 2/3 | Still reminiscing, George raises his glass— | 197' 8" |
| 2:14 | takes drink and— | 201' |
| 2:15 | lowers glass. | 202' 8" |
| 2:16 1/3 | CUT TO Nick, on swing, silent as he studies George. | 204' 4" |
| 2:20 1/3 | Nick (very quietly): "What?" | 210' 8" |
| 2:21 1/3 | Nick clears his throat. | 211' 8" |
| 2:22 2/3 | Nick: "What happened to the boy?" | 213' 14" |
| 2:24 | PAUSE. BACK TO CLOSE-UP of George. George as if in another world. | 216' |
| 2:27 | Nick (o.s.): "The boy who had shot his mother." | 220' 6" |
| 2:28 2/3 | PAUSE. No reaction from George. | 222' 12" |

| Timing | Action | Footage |
|---|---|---|
| 2:31 1/3 | George glances o.s. at Nick. "I won't tell you." | 227' |
| 2:32 1/3 | PAUSE. | 228' 6" |
| 2:33 2/3 | Nick (o.s.): "All right." | 230' 10" |
| 2:34 1/3 | PAUSE. | 231' 12" |
| 2:35 1/3 | George (once more reflects): "The following summer, on a country road, with his learner's permit in his pocket and his father on the front seat to his right, he swerved his car to avoid a porcupine." | 233' |
| 2:43 2/3 | PAUSE. George's eyes widen as if driving car— | 245' 9" |
| 2:45 1/3 | George: "He drove straight into a large tree." | 248' |
| 2:48 | PAUSE. Nick (faintly pleading, o.s.): "No!" | 252' |
| 2:49 | George shakes his head as if to answer. | 253' 8" |
| 2:50 | George: "He wasn't killed, of course, and in the hospital when he was conscious and out of danger, and when they told him his father was—" | 255' |
| 2:58 1/3 | PAUSE. | 267' 10" |
| 2:59 | George: "dead,—he began to laugh, I have been told." | 268' 8" |
| 3:04 | PAUSE. | 276' |
| 3:05 1/3 | George: "His laughter grew and would not stop—" | 278' |
| 3:09 | PAUSE. | 283' 8" |
| 3:10 2/3 | George: "and it was not until that, after they jammed a needle into his arm, not until his consciousness had slipped from him, that his laughter subsided—stopped—" | 286' 4" |
| 3:23 1/3 | PAUSE. | 305' |
| 3:25 1/3 | George: "and when he was recovered from his injuries enough so he could—be moved without damage should he struggle—" | 308' |
| 3:33 | PAUSE. George continues to look down toward ground. | 319' 8" |
| 3:35 | George: "he was put in an asylum." | 322' 8" |

| Timing | Action | Footage |
|---|---|---|
| 3:37 | END of above speech and FIRST MUSIC OUT. | 325' 8" |
| 3:40 | George: "That was thirty years ago." | 330' |
| 3:42 | PAUSE. George raises glass and— | 333' |
| 3:43 1/3 | takes drink and— | 335' 4" |
| 3:44 | lowers glass. Nick (o.s.): "Is he still there?" | 336' 2" |
| 3:45 2/3 | George looks o.s. toward Nick. | 338' 8" |
| 3:47 1/3 | George: "Oh, yes." | 341'4" |
| 3:48 2/3 | PAUSE. George looks forward. | 343' |
| 3:50 | George: "I'm told, for these thirty years—" | 345' |
| 3:52 1/3 | PAUSE. | 348' 10" |
| 3:54 | George: "he's—not uttered—" | 351' |
| 3:55 2/3 | PAUSE. | 353' 11" |
| 3:57 1/3 | George: "one sound." | 356' |
| 4:00 1/3 | SPEECH over. MUSIC OUT as he continues to stare down toward ground. | 360' 8" |
| 4:05 2/3 | CUT TO Nick on swing. | 368' 8" |

The music begins after the crucial line, "and he had killed his mother with a shotgun some years before." The bass clarinet is given a melodic idea that functions as an introduction to the actual beginning of the piece. There is a pause after Burton says, "Bergin and water," and the violins enter on a high C (measure 7). This note is soon joined by other pitches in descending order, and these combine into a sustained chord functioning as a departure point for what follows. (See Ex. III.4a, b.)

The pulsating rhythm, first stated by the violins and transferred to the cellos two measures later, becomes a rhythmic basis for the entire cue. In one sense, this rhythm pushes both the music and the scenario forward. In another, it tends to mark time and unify the sequence, encapsulating the scene into one entity.

About forty-five seconds into this cue, Burton describes how people in

Ex. III.4a.                    *Who's Afraid of Virginia Woolf?*

**Alex North**

Ex. III.4b.

the bar laughed at the boy's use of the word "Bergin": "and the laughter grew." Alex North chooses this point to bring out the pathetic nature of the moment by releasing the high C from its chordal function and by introducing a long, beautifully plaintive melodic line that eventually leads to the C an octave below (measures 12–30). [*The accompaniment to this line appears in two lower voices using the same rhythm mentioned above and written in the style of fourth species counterpoint, involving a series of suspensions in chromatic descent. This produces a relentless descending chromatic chain, which, like the rhythm noted in Ex. III.4a, contributes to the sense of forward motion.*] (See Ex. III.4c.)

Ex. III.4c.

(Accidentals continue in force until
cancelled or changed.)

A particularly poignant moment in the monologue arrives when Burton reflects that the next day each of the boys had a "grown-up's hangover. But it was the grandest day—of my—youth." Notice that North had underlined the word "youth" in the timing sheet (Ex. III.3.). It is clear that he regarded this word as a point in the monologue requiring special attention. The violin line that had moved through an octave, the descending chromatic chain in the accompaniment, and, of course, the pulsating rhythmic pattern work together to prepare for this telling moment in the text. North goes one step further by accenting the word "youth," with a descending fifth in the bass (A♭-D♭) providing a harmonic accent. (See Ex. III.4d.)

Ex. III.4d.

..."youth"

Midway in the monologue, Burton is asked what became of the boy after that night in the gin mill. Burton describes how the boy goes out for a driving lesson with his father, swerves to avoid a porcupine, and hits a tree; his father is killed. The boy ends up in an asylum and has not spoken a word in thirty years. North writes a variation of the first half of the cue for this section, intensifying the music slightly by telescoping the original form and thickening the texture through the use of additional contrapuntal lines (measures 35–55). Unfortunately, the short five-measure coda at the end of the cue is not used in the prints of the film I have seen.

In summation, at least three factors in the music make a dramatic contribution to the success of this long scene: the extended top line in the violins; the chromatic chain of suspensions in the accompaniment, which by nature keeps reaching forward; and the pulsating rhythm that acquires a subtle momentum of its own. (See Ex. III.5.)

Ex. III.5.          *Who's Afraid of Virginia Woolf?*

## "Bergin"

**Alex North**

*(continued)*

*(continued)*

(continued)

*(continued)*

## Synchronization

A musical beat or pulse in synchronization with an event can bring about an unwanted effect. For instance, suppose a man playfully jabs his umbrella into the stomach of the person he is talking to. If the beat in the music coincides with the jabbing, the event would seem predetermined and not as playful. To take a more obvious situation, imagine a happy man walking down the street. He could easily be made to look ridiculous if the accompanying music were in the same tempo as his walking pace.

In *Fool for Love,* the situation demanded music wherein the pulse would be evident, though discreet, but under no circumstances could the musical beat be in synchronization with ambient sounds. In this scene, Kim Basinger is visibly collecting herself after a verbal battle with Sam Shepard, and we see her walking back to the motel. Robert Altman, who often has a healthy disdain for the characters in his movies, suggested that I think of her as a "defeated soldier in the Civil War trudging home."[12] That was exactly the kind of direction I needed.

I decided to begin the music with a slow-moving progression of block chords that would become the harmonic basis for the rest of the cue. The musical pulse was not readily discernible, but the entrance of each chord provided an ictus of sorts, and that was all that was required at the onset. However, any synchronization between the chords and the sound of Basinger's footsteps had to be avoided, or the serious nature of the scene would have been compromised. Ordinarily, it is a simple matter to time the sound of footsteps and to arrive at a musical tempo that will not duplicate the ambient sound. In this case, however, Basinger's walk on the gravel was uneven, and the slow crunching sound of each footstep lacked definition. We experimented until we found a tempo that satisfied all the conditions. Here the quarter note equaled 52.13!

Twenty-four seconds into the cue at the end of Basinger's walk, the camera cuts to a little girl, then back to Basinger. Later, the two embrace. In the story, the girl is Basinger at a younger age; showing them in the same frame brings the past and the present together.

For the child, I introduced a melodic idea played by the piano in the high register, which moved in fairly steady eighth-note patterns producing a musical pulse. Thus, once the melodic line comes in and is continued, the tempo permeates the remainder of the scene—precisely what we wanted. (See Ex. III.6.)

Though a simultaneity of ambient sound with the musical beat often has to be avoided, there are times when this kind of simultaneity is effective. For instance, during the main titles of *Judgment at Nuremberg* (1961), flags bearing the Nazi insignia flash on the screen with some regularity, and in synchronization with the musical beat. Gold explains his approach:

I wanted those bits of the swastika to have more of an impact than they did visually. They didn't have any sound, of course, and I found that I could have a slow and menacing march at a tempo that would correspond with these things flashed on the screen. When I showed the cutter what I had in mind, he accommodated me by moving the flags around so that all were in synchronization with the beat. Other-

Ex. III.6.                                  *Fool for Love*

# May and the Little Girl

George Burt

*(continued)*

(continued)

wise, the momentum would have been disturbed and I would have had to pull away from the picture, neither of which was good.[13]

Gold brings up an interesting point regarding objects that suddenly appear or fall but do not make a sound. A falling feather, for instance, settles without making an audible sound. Composers describe this effect as "rub-

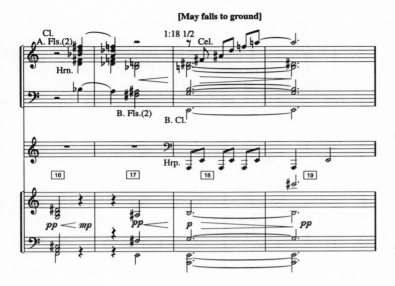

bery." How this effect is treated musically—whether it is given a musical accent of sorts—depends entirely upon its importance within a situation.

The musical pulse or beat, then, can have a decisive function in the overall impact, vitality, and meaning of a sequence. The acting may be superlative; the camera work, photography, cutting, and set design perfect. However, without music, the action or story may feel incomplete, missing something that is not achievable by the visible theater alone. This can be an audible pulse of some sort, achievable only through musical means.

## Pacing

There is an old joke about the different ways movies are made in various countries. In Germany, for example, you can show cloud formations for three minutes, then a plane, followed by a story. In England, you show a cloud formation and within thirty seconds there must be a plane. In the United States, you show the cloud and in the first ten seconds the plane has to crash!

To be sure, pacing in film is, to some extent, a cultural matter, and in the restless milieu of the twentieth century, many people become uneasy if something isn't happening all the time. This expectation becomes a problem for a commercialized art form that depends almost entirely on gate receipts for survival. There are many in the industry who are convinced that if each scene isn't highlighted in some way, people won't come to the theater. Thus, many films, especially those lacking a substantial basis for development, inevitably lean toward or invite exaggerated detail; whereas other films, particularly those with a strong story line, can afford to lead up to a point without relying upon intermittent overstatement to sustain interest. Here, the details in and of themselves have a sufficient persuasive quality of their own; the importance of their integrative function within an observable larger design does the trick.

*The Lyrical Approach*

An overall problem for the composer is to ensure that a point of climax in a situation as well as in the entire film is not reached too soon and that the meaning behind the action is suitably addressed. In many cases involving an extended climactic or action-oriented scene, composers have decided against supplying music that is conspicuously disjunct, chordal, or rhythmic in style and have instead chosen to introduce music that is distinctly melodic in character, music that has a lyrical quality.

The lyrical quality of music can be used to establish a sense of motion that leads up to an action functioning as a climactic moment. For example, near the end of *The Young Lions,* there is a night scene in which three men are caught behind enemy lines, and it is terribly important that their effort to find their way back to their own side is paced in such a way that a feeling of controlled anxiety is kept in the foreground of the sequence. Because of the confusion in the ranks of both sides, the men are in constant danger of being fired upon not only by the Germans but also by their own troops. To reach the Allied camp, they must cross the river undetected and then emphatically identify themselves as Americans. The lyrical way in which Hugo Friedhofer's music deepens the effect of the scene and paces it so that there is a gradual but sustained build-up to the climax makes an impact. Friedhofer's handling of this situation is exemplary.

The music begins with an ostinato-like constant quarter-note idea quietly expressed by bass clarinets and played legato as the men work their way through the underbrush. This idea quickly identifies both with the nighttime and with the men's determination to reach their destination. As they approach the river's edge, Friedhofer adds to the quarter-note idea a slow-moving chorale for muted trumpets and flutes that ties in with the threatening nature of what the men are up against, and this helps set the tone as the river comes into view. [*The chorale, based on quartel harmony implicit in the quarter-note idea, is transferred to high strings a few measures later, an orchestrational detail that opens up both the registral range of the music and the feeling of the shot. (See measure 5.)*]

The men receive a sudden burst of fire, and they dive over the side of the riverbank for cover. This action is given only a slight accent in the strings (see measure 9), possibly because there is sufficient ambient noise to make the point. In the meantime, the strings and brass continue to alternate up to where dialogue begins (see measure 13). [*Notice that the bass line has moved between the pitches E, D, and C. To underline the beginning of the dialogue and to provide a sense of arrival, Friedhofer continues the line on to B.*] The quarter-note idea is abandoned momentarily as the men argue about crossing the river, but a few seconds later Friedhofer eloquently brings in a quiet statement of the main titles theme (discussed in Chapter 2) to suggest a sense of unbridled determination previously associated with that theme (see measures 15–30). This section of music, with the theme in low clarinets and horns, tends to focus on the undeniable fact that the river has to be crossed regardless of the danger.

When two of the men start swimming—the third remains on shore—Friedhofer returns to the quarter-note idea in the bass clarinet, reestablishing the sense of motion. This continues until the camera cuts to a view of the opposite shore (see measure 39). Note that in counterpoint to the quarter-note idea, Friedhofer also brings back the slow-moving chorale, which alternates between brass and strings. The tension between the chords and the quarter-note idea supports the feeling that, at this point, the soldiers pass every inch of the way at a painfully slow rate. Ironically, the river's quietness seems more treacherous with the inclusion of the chorale progression in high strings. When this idea is transferred from strings to brass and back again, a sense of desperation evolves—partly, I think, through the straightforward alternation of timbres. (See Ex. III.7.)

Ex. III.7.                        *The Young Lions*

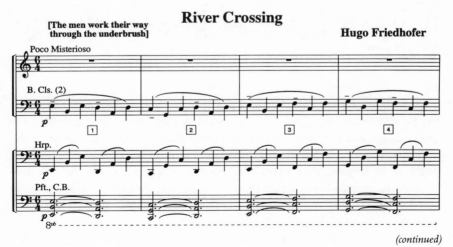

(continued)

*(continued)*

Preparation for the high point of the "River Crossing" is achieved virtually by musical means alone—not necessarily aided by what appears on the screen. This is where the camera cuts from the swimmers to a shot of the opposite shore—their destination. It is a low-lit shot that doesn't have much of an impact. But Friedhofer introduces a particularly plaintive line for woodwinds and horns that dramatically intensifies the moment. A few seconds later, the swimmers enter the frame and struggle toward the riverbank (see measures 39–42).

[Ackerman: "We got to swim across" (to reach their troops)]

[Another man argues, "we'll be picked off," and besides, "I can't swim."]

[The non-swimmer retreats into bushes]

(continued)

*(continued)*

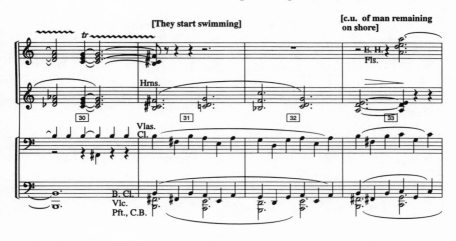

(continued)

*(continued)*

Finally, the men find a place to climb ashore, rest a moment, and then start running inland, not knowing what they will encounter. Friedhofer goes against this treacherous moment by recapitulating the soft-spoken chorale along with the quarter-note idea. By means of contrast, he prepares for the climactic end of the scene, when the men are suddenly and mistakenly fired upon by their own troops. One of the men is hit, and the cue comes to a close on a sustained dissonant-sounding A-minor triad over a G$^\sharp$ in the bass.

*(continued)*

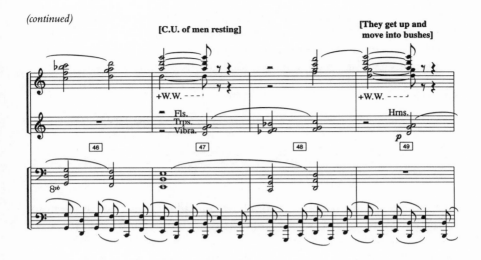

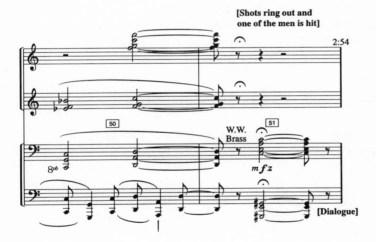

## Reiterated Rhythmic Patterns

Composers of both concert and film music frequently have employed a reiterated rhythmic figure to intensify an extended passage of music. The "Danses des Adolescentes" from Stravinsky's *The Rite of Spring* instantly comes to mind. An example of this technique in film music occurs in Bernard Herrmann's cue for the final scene of *Obsession* (1969), which, over a period of more than a minute or so, builds to the ending shot.

In this scene, Cliff Robertson walks quickly through an airline terminal. For many reasons he is near-crazed at this point, and Herrmann introduces a rhythmic pattern for timpani and lower strings that quickly picks up on Robertson's intense inner agitation. (See Ex. III.8.)

Ex. III.8.                          *Obsession*

**Bernard Herrmann**

As Robertson breaks into a run, Herrmann adds a cluster of organ notes to the rhythmic pattern, which amplifies the blinding, unfocused nature of his "obsession." At this point, a problem of pacing arises: Robertson's run through the terminal is a long sequence. A continuation of the same rhythmic pattern, accented by timpani, would eventually become tedious and distracting. Herrmann's solution? He backs off slightly and presents subtle variants of the four-measure grouping.

*Suspended Time*

A repeated rhythmic pattern can intensify a situation. Also, as noted in our discussion of "Bergin" from *Who's Afraid of Virginia Woolf?* (above), a repeated rhythm has a pulsating effect that, in terms of pacing, tends to mark time. There are occasions, however, that call for an entirely different effect: where the music must create a feeling of suspended time, ruling out the feeling of time as measured by a clock . The score to *Fantastic Voyage* (1966) is a good example. The significance of the musical approach in this film is that the story takes place in real time. That is, all the events in the film occur within a time span equal to the length of the film—roughly an hour and a half. Because the script continuously makes reference to this fact, Rosenman was in a position to counter the notion of real time and to concentrate on other aspects of the inner drama.

Rosenman wrote an intense and contemporary score for *Fantastic Voyage*. The futuristic aspect of the film (directed by Richard Fleischer) lent itself to this treatment. Rosenman recalls that "a producer asked me to write a jazz score, and I asked him why. He said that he wanted the picture to be the first hip science fiction movie. I said that's a great idea for an advertising agency, but it doesn't fit the film. The producer was later dismissed from the project, by the way, but that is another matter."[14]

The most compelling aspect of the score is that it consists almost entirely of multileveled clusters of sound. Downbeats or arrival points of various kinds are generally avoided in the score. Where they do exist, they are downplayed. Highly contrasting material, such as differentiating and easily discernible thematic ideas, is also generally avoided. A gradual change of texture is preferred to the patterned emergence of a sustained melodic shape, which would impose beginnings and endings. The articulative process in Rosenman's score emerges with the gentle shifting of orchestral colors, dissonant levels, and textures. The overall effect heightens the expressive content of the film in juxtaposition with its "real time" component and intensifies the otherworldliness of the moment by creating a sense of floating buoyancy.

The first third of the picture attends to the story line, detailing and outlining the problem and the solution. The plan is to miniaturize a submarine and its crew so they can be injected into the bloodstream of a patient requiring surgery. The music is first introduced as the sub breaks into the bloodstream, and the massive sound of the opening musical gesture brings the audience into immediate contact with the expansive nature of the voyage. One of the characters says, "Man is the center of the universe. We stand in the middle of infinity . . . between inner and outer space." Indeed, the score's accumulating layers of musical sound both establish and sustain the feeling of suspension in space and in time.

The opening gesture is based on a succession of pitches encompassing two and a half octaves. These combine into a cluster that becomes a harmonic basis for the score. About sixty seconds later Rosenman introduces a four-note motivic idea that recurs throughout the score at critical points. (See Ex. III.9a, b.)

Ex. III.9a.                    *Fantastic Voyage*

**Leonard Rosenman**

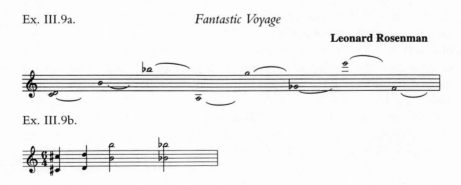

Ex. III.9b.

When the submarine reaches its destination—the brain—Rosenman introduces what might be described as a chorale tune for trumpet accompanied by an extremely complex and constantly shifting harmonic texture. By association, this chorale tune dramatizes the sense of arrival. (See Ex. III.9c.)

Ex. III.9c.

That these melodic ideas occur in the *Voyage* score does not in any way mitigate the previous point that an avoidance of discernible thematic material contributes to the sense of timelessness in the music. On the contrary, these ideas tend to throw the overriding impact of the score into momentary relief, rendering the thrust of style and intent of the score with a deeper sense of meaning.

A similar situation occurs in *2001: A Space Odyssey*. Alex North was hired to write the score for the memorable film, but at the last moment, after the score had been written, Kubrick decided to use preexisting music. This was a most unfortunate development, since North's outstanding score would have contributed so much of a highly personal nature to the film. The music works within the full range of nobility and elegance, strength and insightfulness. It is memorable and lasting. Happily, a recording of North's score was released recently on compact disc (Saraband Records, 1993) and, after twenty years, it finally can be heard. However, it can be said that Kubrick's choice of music does have merit with respect to what music can offer to a film of this kind. Near the beginning of the film, Kubrick uses "The Blue Danube" waltz, which provides a lyrical edge loaded with earthbound associations. The music heightens a sense of direction and purpose in accompaniment to shots of a shuttle on its way to a space station. But when the mission to Jupiter begins and earth ties are more or less severed, Kubrick uses choral music by György Ligeti. In this music, a sea of voices in cluster-like formations suggests a vacuum having no apparent boundaries. Unlike "The Blue Danube," which has a decisive pulse in triple meter, metrical pulse in the Ligeti is omitted altogether. The music is in response to, and thus corroborates and paces, the intended feeling for this sequence, in which the suspension of time and a sense of endlessness are vital.

*Real Time*

Totally different situations occur in films in which music is needed to emphasize the passage of time—situations in which every passing second becomes an essential aspect of the story. For instance, the climactic scene in *High Noon* (1952), which assumably takes place in real time, uses the hands of the clock as a visual reminder that less and less time remains for fateful decisions. The editing in the memorable scene one minute before the arrival of the train points this up. There is a sequence of shots, each held for a little over three seconds, in which the camera focuses first on the clock, then on Gary Cooper, the outlaws, the train tracks, the church, the saloon, the empty streets, and so on. The music consists of a variant of the "Clementine" theme accompanied by a heavy, pulsating beat brought out by timpani, pizzicato strings, and, eventually, brass. The beat corresponds with the second hand on the clock (sped up by the editors, in this case) to dramatize the crush of experience as it is crowded into an instant.

*The Active Voice*

In a much broader context, pacing is a special issue in *Tora! Tora! Tora!* (1970). This extraordinary picture, directed by Richard Fleischer, is more than two hours long and differs from most dramas in that the ending (that is, the attack on Pearl Harbor) is already known. The situation demands an approach to the dramatic curve that allows for a gradual rise of intensity over the very long time span leading to the attack. Jerry Goldsmith's approach is notable: the music fulfills every requirement.

The first third of the picture addresses the development of the Japanese plan for the attack; the United States is asleep at the wheel. The main titles music, which is distinctly Japanese in its melodic and rhythmic style, thus corresponds with the active voice in the narrative. (See Ex. III.10.)

This theme, first stated by the koto (a Japanese string instrument), is repeated by other instruments and finally by whole sections of the orchestra. The music builds to a climax in the main titles and thus makes a definitive comment about the explosive nature of the situation, as regards the strength and determination of the Japanese. Cuts from the Americans to the Japanese in the first part of the picture bring out an essential element: The Americans, at this point, react passively to the threat of war, whereas the Japanese are filled with a sense of purpose. To dramatize this distinction, Goldsmith wrote music that is stylistically assertive for the scenes in Japan, while generally omitting music altogether for shots showing the humdrum

Ex. III.10.　　　　　　　　*Tora! Tora! Tora!*

**Main Titles Theme**

**Jerry Goldsmith**

Koto--Baritone--Baritone with Orchestra--French horns--(Interlude)--Trombones--Strings and Winds

daily life in the United States. This approach not only corresponds to our dismay with the American side over its countless errors in judgment in contrast to the highly spirited sense of direction exemplified by the Japanese, but also allows for a more gradual build-up to the attack than would have been the case had music been included in the scenes representing the American side as well.

Once the plan for the Pearl Harbor attack is formulated and unveiled to high-ranking Japanese officers, arguments with respect to its advisability begin to emerge. A sequence of scenes brings out the disparity of opinion at the highest possible levels. It is a turning point in the drama, and Goldsmith expertly pulls away from the positive spirit and moves into the darker areas of dissent and concern. Admiral Yamamoto urges Japan's prime minister to pursue negotiations with Washington, but the prime minister shows little interest in this suggestion. For this scene, Goldsmith composes slowly evolving clusters of synthesized sound combined with fragments from the main theme performed on the koto. The effect is one of dread and hopelessness.

The next scene takes place in Washington's Japanese Embassy. The Japanese ambassador complains that Tokyo has ignored his "repeated inquiries" for a reply to the "compromise proposals offered by Secretary Hull." He fears that the war he has "dreaded for so long may soon become a reality."

It is a somber scene, and Goldsmith writes a variant of the main theme for low strings over a tonic pedal in C minor.

After a cut to Secretary Hull's office, for which music is omitted, there is a pivotal scene in which Admiral Yamamoto addresses his officers. He informs them that negotiations are still taking place and that "if a special solution is found, the fleet will be recalled at once." The music consists of the theme played by low horns doubled with bass flute, over a tonic pedal in G minor, in combination with synthesized clusters. Alarmed at Yamamoto's statement, one of the officers says, "Once at sea, to turn back would be a disgrace." Yamamoto vehemently reacts and says in no uncertain terms: "If any commander here is inclined to reject an order to return when the path to peace is open—let him resign—now!" Yamamoto's words easily carry the shot. No music is needed. But as the camera backs away from a tight shot of him to a wide shot of the stony-faced officers, the music returns, this time in C minor. In a slow, plodding tempo, the music concludes the scene at funereal pace. The shift in tonality, from G minor to C minor, helps delineate the two plateaus of this somber scene.

The point? By pulling back from the high-spirited style in the first section of the film and allowing the music to correspond with the anguished despair expressed by the dissenting members of the Japanese forces, Goldsmith puts himself in a good position to reintensify the music for subsequent scenes that precede the actual attack. In this manner, the emotional curve within the larger design comes into focus.

*Point of Release*

The attack on Pearl Harbor in *Tora! Tora! Tora!* was, of course, the focal point or moment of dramatic release, in which all elements within the story converged. Music was not used for the battle, nor was it needed. Ambient sound alone was sufficient to carry the scenes. More important, the drama was over at that point. What remained was the attack itself, which was, of course, of epic proportions.

The point of release is absolutely crucial to the dramatic shape of any story. Generally, it refers to that moment when things come together, when various strands of the conflict are picked up and dealt with in some way. It can be a very emotional moment, when there is a sense of relief as the reasons for conflict are resolved. (The six–four chord is often kept in reserve for such moments.) Or it can represent the time for action, when such becomes inevitable. This was the case in *Tora! Tora! Tora!* and in the cue "Desperate Journey" for *Between Heaven and Hell* (discussed earlier in this chapter), to mention just two instances.

Earlier in the book it was mentioned that directors must have a feeling for overall shape, not just for detail. Much the same should be said about composers—especially with regard to how the point of release is approached musically and how it is dealt with when it arrives. It is disastrous when certain scenes leading up to the release are overstated; the actual release then becomes anticlimactic. It is equally disastrous when the release point is given far more prominence than it deserves. This immediately reduces the film to a low form, which will lose at least part of the audience. In any case, the better or more experienced film composers treat these moments with extreme care. A point of release may or may not require music, but it certainly has a decisive influence on the score and on the question of pacing throughout.

In his music for *The Misfits*, Alex North was faced with a special problem with respect to the point of release. We will look at the sequence that occurs in the last third of the film, when Guido (Eli Wallach) flies his biplane through the canyons of Nevada in search of wild mustangs. All elements of the story converge at this time.

To understand the reason music was required for this sequence and the demands this made on the score, it is necessary to take a broad view of the overall dramatic structure. But first, let us consider the nature of the conflict involved. John Huston, who directed the film, put it succinctly: "It is about people who sell their work but won't sell themselves. Anybody who holds out—is a misfit." In the 1930s, Gay Langland, a Reno cowboy (played by Clark Gable), survived by rounding up wild mustangs and selling them as riding ponies or workhorses. After the war the mustangs were used for dog food, which puts a different, negative stamp on Langland's work. On a certain level, then, "this movie is about a world in change. Before World War II, he [Gay Langland] was noble. Now [after the war], he is ignoble. He's the same man but the world has changed."[15]

The film divides into three sections or acts. In the first act (discussed in Chapter 2 in connection with source music), Langland meets Roslyn (Marilyn Monroe), and after an evening of drinks, the two move in together. North said that for this section of the film, "I want to first establish the character of this town and then [write] a simple lonely theme for Roslyn. I think we can afford to play against the changes of mood and still continue a musical thought."[16] Recognizing that the plot details had many implications, North did not want the music to be disruptive or, worse yet, bring undue emphasis to any particular idea.

The second act begins with the four characters (Gable, Wallach, Monroe, and Thelma Ritter) driving to Dayton, Nevada, for a rodeo. They meet

Perse (Montgomery Clift) and persuade him to join them in a roundup of mustangs. Huston was "against any outside musical comment for this act. If they're playing some God-awful hoe-down music in the bar, that might be the best comment."[17] North agreed and wrote mostly source music. But at the point where Perse is talking with Roslyn and begins to reflect on painful thoughts of his mother, North gently moves from the music in the bar to a quiet statement of the main titles theme (cited in Chapter 2). Here the theme is used to bring out the catalytic nature of Roslyn's role in the film.

North summed up his approach to the first two acts:

We will have a contrast of theme and variations [in association with Roslyn's role] against the mood of this town. The source music should be interwoven against the personal music. The only thing I'm trying to avoid is "cue" music, where music comes on a specific line. I hear a thin, angular kind of musical statement during those moments of reflection on Roslyn's part, and no significant statement until the last third of the picture.[18]

To be sure, the third act brings the play to a climax, when everything is confronted head-on. It stands apart from the other two acts.

As Arthur Miller conceived it, the third act begins with a shot from Guido's plane as he approaches the top of a mountain range. The others have just waved him off. It is his job to fly past the mountains and into the canyon to find the mustangs and herd them back to camp. Miller: "The whole picture has been blown through a horn and there on the ridge is where the horn bellows out. Somewhere there is where you start the blast. The characters are stripped naked."[19] In this third act, the men are locked into a struggle with the wildness of the mustangs, and with the meaning of their own lives.

North recalls that for this section he "tried to go above the personalized music and do something in a more universal sense—man's triumph over nature, man's attempt to prove virility—the music had to take on the form of greater abstraction and detachment."[20] In a most emphatic way, North's energetic symphonic score for this long sequence works within the firm belief that something of an overriding or grandiose nature is taking place.

The cue entitled "Roundup" is brought in at the instant Guido's plane becomes airborne. [*An accented high $G^\flat$ against a sustained F in the strings has an unsettling feeling, which is given greater breadth by a subsequent entrance of low strings and brass filling in a superimposed major and minor $B^\flat$ harmony. The horns follow with an ascending line, leading up to an $A^\flat$ or lowered seventh degree, intensifying the harmonic function* *of B♭. This introductory passage then ends on a G♭-minor triad (with a major seventh, ninth, and conflicting major third), which prepares for and is resolved by the structural downbeat on F at measure 10. This held dissonant-sounding chord in measures 7–9 corresponds with the moment the plane approaches the mountain peak that Guido must negotiate in order to reach an open valley, his destination. A sweeping scalar gesture in the Phrygian mode of G♭ intensifies the moment as the plane passes over the mountain peak.*

The principal section of "Roundup" begins with measure 10, as Guido's plane swoops into the valley. This is the point that North has been waiting for all along. He writes a fully concerted movement for orchestra that enlarges upon the deep sense of release underlying not only this moment but also the significance of the sequence in the context of the entire film. For these men, the time for action, not words, has finally arrived. (See Ex. III.11.)

[*The most immediate aspect of the music for "Roundup" derives from the asymmetric 5/8 meter, divided into groups of 2+3. Asymmetry appears within phrase structures as well. For instance, the first phrase (measures 10–23) divides into measure-length groupings of (in 3/8) 3+3+4+ (in 3/4) 4. Like a loose cannon, the feeling of metrical unpredictability fuses the sequence with a raw sense of high energy, enlarging upon what appears on the screen.*

[*The repeated-note motivic idea (a) at measure 10 in the horns is brought back many times and becomes a source for subsequent derived ideas. The falling fifth (E–A) (b) in the violins at measure 17 comes from this idea, as does the rising, stepwise figure beginning with measure 30 (c).*

[*The extension of (c) into two measures becomes a melodic unit that is embedded in other phrases: measures 48–60 and 95–108. The horn line beginning with measure 81 is derived from motive (c) in augmentation and is extended to become an additional melodic idea. Notice how key events in the film are in correspondence with structural articulations in the music. Beginning with measure 104, North brings back the main titles theme, subtly stated in the bass register. This provides an ironic touch to shots of the plane buzzing the mustangs.*]

To one extent or another, many scenes in film identify with a particular mode of experience within a time continuum. Cause and effect is one such mode. The "River Crossing" from *The Young Lions* and the overall approach to *Tora! Tora! Tora!* come close to working within this frame of reference. On the other hand, when the crush of experience is crowded into an instant, we experience a different mode of time. The examples from *High Noon* and *Obsession* serve as illustrations. When there appears to be a feeling of indeterminacy in the flow of life, where everything is filled with multiple meanings without any apparent structure, we experience time from still another point of view. *Fantastic Voyage* and *2001* come to mind as examples.

On the matter of pacing as it is experienced by the viewer in the movie theater, Montague comments, "If no shot is wrongly chosen or shown for

Ex. III.11.                              *The Misfits*

# Roundup

Alex North

*(continued)*

so long that the thread of his interest snaps, if each shot appears to answer exactly his unspoken, felt but not yet formulated, curiosity, he will feel that he is participating in the event portrayed."[21] Pacing is a fundamental problem in all films. Music plays no small part in the solution to this problem.

*(continued)*

(continued)

*(continued)*

[Mustangs come
into view]

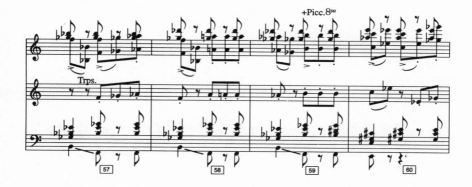

*(continued)*

*(continued)*

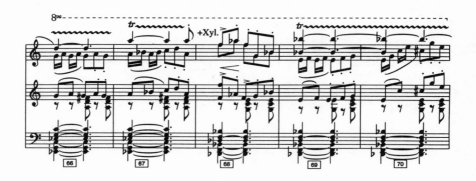

[Plane buzzes mustangs]

[l.s. of plane banking
at 90° angle]

*(continued)*

*(continued)*

(M.T.'s Theme)

(continued)

*(continued)*

## Chapter Four

# The Sequence as a Unit

Until now, we have isolated various aspects and functions of film music to explore their individual applications and importance within given contexts. In this chapter, we will examine three well-known sequences. In each case, we will see how the music is responsive to a wide range of simultaneous needs.

## *The Best Years of Our Lives:* Homecoming Scene

Probably one of the most significant and most often discussed film scores is Hugo Friedhofer's music for *The Best Years of Our Lives* (mentioned in Chapter 2), a landmark in film music. We look now at the "Homecoming" cue.

*Best Years* was written by Pulitzer Prize–winning playwright Robert Sherwood, directed by William Wyler, and photographed by cinematographer Gregg Toland (*Citizen Kane*). The story, inspired by a *Time* magazine article (August 1944), takes place at the end of World War II. It is the saga of three veterans from different socioeconomic backgrounds who return to the United States to face readjustment to civilian life. The principal roles are played by Fredric March, Myrna Loy, Dana Andrews, and non-actor Harold Russell, who was unforgettable in the role of the amputee.

The three men meet for the first time as they hitch a ride aboard a B–17 to Boone City, their hometown. They eventually fall asleep during the long trip. The music begins as Homer, the amputee, first wakes up, before the others do. It continues as the plane lands and accompanies their subsequent cab ride from the air base. The music ends after Homer is dropped off at his house. The scene is divided into four sections: 1. Dawn, 2. Boone City

143

(as it is first viewed from the plane), 3. Taxi Ride, and 4. Arrival at Homer's House. The music not only consists of key elements vital to the story line but also details the transition from the plane to Homer's house. In one continuous gesture, the music delineates and binds together all these aspects.

The first section, "Dawn," opens with a panoramic view of the clouds seen from the nose of the plane. The men are asleep. [*Friedhofer begins with a statement and canonic extension of the minor third idea (x in Ex. II.10).*] The canonic extension allows for a gradual opening up of the scene, providing a sense of anticipation. The music is played in a relatively slow tempo, marked "*modto con grandezza*" in the original score. Homer awakes and looks out the window at the grandeur of the dawn as the music comes to a cadence with a chordal progression (y in Ex. II.10) in D major (measures 9–10). (See Ex. IV.1.)

At the end of the shot, the camera holds on Homer for nearly twenty seconds—a long time for a close-up (c.u.)—and it becomes clear that his incertitude runs far deeper than he is ready to admit. Homer has lost both hands in the war and dreads his girlfriend Wilma's reaction to his artificial ones. Earlier he has said in passing: "Wilma's only a kid. She's never seen anything like these hooks." The music is of vital importance during this close-up. By combining the broad quality of the *Best Years* theme with a suggestion of the soulful "Neighbors" theme (measures 10–14), Friedhofer builds on a depth of feeling in recognition of Homer's inner thoughts. It is a touching moment that is both moving and private.

There is a dissolve to the next morning, and the three men, now fully awake, are staring intently through the nose of the plane as it approaches their destination. This begins the second section, and Friedhofer electrifies the moment by introducing an exuberant "Boone City" theme. The music is written in a style that connects with both the busy feeling of a city and the excitement of coming home.

For purposes of experimentation, let us consider an alternative musical approach to this section before we look at what Friedhofer did. It should become clear that Friedhofer's approach captures a feeling that brings the entire sequence into dramatic focus.

We know all three men are apprehensive about returning to civilian life. Earlier, Al (Fredric March) had obliquely referred to this in conversation with Fred (Dana Andrews).

Fred:   Remember what it felt like when you went overseas?
Al:     As well as I remember my own name.

Ex. IV.1.                    *The Best Years of Our Lives*

## Dawn Shot

**Hugo Friedhofer**

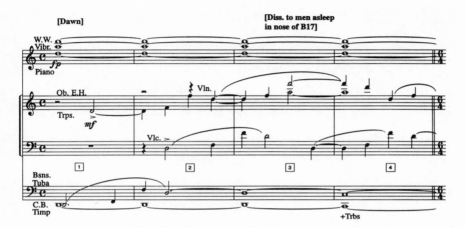

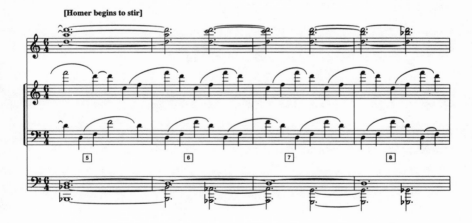

*(continued)*

Fred:   I feel the same way now, only more so.

Al:     The thing that scares me most is that everybody's going to
        try to . . . rehabilitate me.

The music for the second section, "Boone City," might have tied in with
this feeling of apprehension, and if Friedhofer had chosen to play it this

*(continued)*

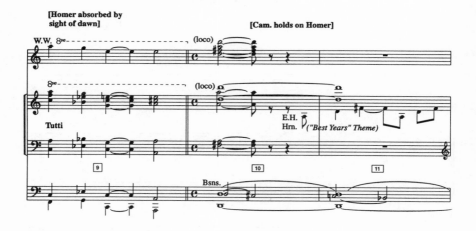

way, he would have been in an excellent position to do so. He could have continued with a kind of quiet variant of the *Best Years* theme (begun, somberly, a few measures back) and, perhaps with high strings, stayed with it until the next section, "Taxi Ride," which depicts the hustle and bustle of the city. Clearly, the "Taxi Ride" scene would then have called for a more ebullient musical style.

To a degree, this alternative approach could have worked, and it would have been an obvious thing to do. It would have tied in with much of the dialogue, especially as the men express their dismay at the sight of hundreds of war planes being converted to scrap.

But Friedhofer opted for another solution, a subtext (a supra reality) that reflected their excitement. Earlier, in the plane during the night:

Fred:    How long since you've been home?
Al:      Uh, a couple of centuries.

This dry comment is in direct contrast to the way they later press forward to catch their first glimpse of the city. Friedhofer's music particularizes and subsequently prolongs this instance of promise, the excitement of coming home, throughout the "Boone City" and "Taxi Ride" sections; as will be seen, he keeps the more or less somber music in reserve for the fourth section, "Arrival," where it is really needed.

*Motivic Reiteration and Prolongation*

The opening four measures of the Allegro (measures 15–18) relate to the shot of the three men staring through the nose of the plane. Friedhofer introduces the beginning motive of the "Boone City" theme, which is first stated by oboe and trumpet and subsequently repeated in different parts of the orchestra. One of the men says, "Boy, the old hometown hasn't changed much, has it?" On this line, Friedhofer brings in a unfolding triad idea that through extensive motivic reiteration functions as a musical prolongation in correspondence with the way they seem to be holding their breath (measures 19–24). As they sight the golf course, Friedhofer inserts a brief statement of the "Boone City" motive in this passage but immediately returns to the hustle of the triadic idea (measures 25–30). (See Ex. IV.2.)

*Harmonic Prolongation*

Significantly, the entire passage thus far appears on the dominant of G major, heightening an expectation for a resolution to the tonic. This brings out an element of irony implicit in the dialogue. One of the men points out the window and says, "People playing golf . . . just as if nothing had happened." As he finishes the line the music resolves to the tonic in G major (measure 31), and the feeling of arrival is firmed up with the first complete statement of the "Boone City" theme (measures 31–47). It is important to take note of the technique employed for this situation—that is, harmonic prolongation (the extension of a harmony that demands resolution) and release (the resolution) which enables Friedhofer to put off the feeling of psychological arrival until the men have had the chance to absorb their first impressions.

Ex. IV.2.                          *The Best Years of Our Lives*

# Boone City

Hugo Friedhofer

(continued)

*(continued)*

["Hey, that must be the new airport."]

all Vlns.

Cls.

50    51    52    53

Hrp. +Timp    +Timp    +Timp

8 Vln.

54    55    56    57

+Timp

[l.s. scrap heap of WW II airplanes]

["I never knew there was so many airplanes."]

W.W. Pft.

Hrns.

pizz.

58    59    60    61

Bsns. (sust.)

(continued)

*(continued)*

(continued)

(continued)

As the plane flies over the Jackson High football field, Homer, the amputee, says, "I wish I had a dollar for every forward pass I threw down there."
And when the camera cuts to a long shot (l.s.) of the football field,
Friedhofer brings in a fragment of the *Best Years* theme, connecting the
music with Homer's injury (measures 47–50). It should be noted that the
"Boone City" theme was derived from the *Best Years* theme, providing a
subtle thematic connection between fundamental elements of the sequence. (See Ex. IV.3.)


Ex. IV.3.                    *The Best Years of Our Lives*

Next, the men catch sight of the "new airport," and, again, Friedhofer draws on the inherent prolongational function of the unfolding triad idea (measures 51–58) in anticipation of the landing. But the "scrap heap" soon comes into view, showing hundreds of World War II planes being readied for "junk." Fred (Dana Andrews), who served as a bombardier, reflects, "What we could have done with them in '43." The music lingers on this line. It is a moment of truth for the men, and Friedhofer subdues the exuberant feeling of the rising, unfolding triads by using the inverted form in augmentation (measures 63–74).

When Fred jumps up and says, "We better get out of the nose while he [the pilot] sets her down" (measure 83), Friedhofer instantly brings back the original form of the unfolding triad idea as a prolongation of the dominant of B major in preparation for the next section.

The "Taxi Ride" section is less problematic than the preceding, since it consists mainly of an interesting succession of familiar "every city" sights: a ballpark, teenagers in a souped-up car, girls waiting for a bus, a hot dog stand, a Woolworth's sign, the firehouse. The exuberance of the "Boone City" theme juxtaposed with the unfolding triad material carries the sequence. Modulations to A♭ and E♭ along the way accent various shots. (See Ex. IV.4.)

Toward the end of the "Taxi Ride" section (measure 138), Homer points to a tavern, "Butch's Place," and laughingly explains that Butch is his uncle. It is a nervous laugh, however, as he is well aware that the cab is approaching his street. Friedhofer has to move away from the prior exuberance of the "Boone City" music to prepare for the next section: "Arrival at Homer's House." It is a challenge to preserve the connection between the two scenes (as they flow together visually) and still make a dramatic shift to a new feeling in the music. In this instance, Friedhofer composed a written *ritard* (in which durational values of notes are lengthened) leading up to a *poco ritard* (in which the tempo is slowed down) (measures 156–57), all of which modulates from E♭ to C major. Significantly, the modulation itself is uncomplicated and the music moves easily into the next key area. Such moments can be mangled by unnecessary complexity of harmonic detail. (See Ex. IV.5.)

Ex. IV.4.                        *The Best Years of Our Lives*

# Taxi Ride

Hugo Friedhofer

*(continued)*

*(continued)*

(continued)

*(continued)*

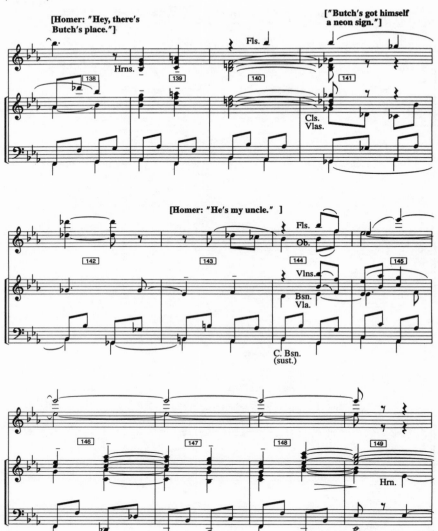

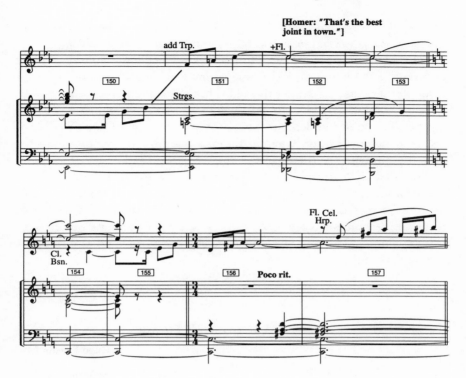

Ex. IV.5.                        *The Best Years of Our Lives*

The fourth section, "Arrival," begins as the cab turns onto Homer's street. There is a complete change of mood, and to tie in with this, Friedhofer introduces the "Neighbors" theme, which has a plaintive and subdued quality (measures 158–67). In addition, the bichordal setting of this theme, D major over C major, is suggestive of an ambivalence that is in agreement with Homer's reluctance to face his family and his girlfriend. [*We would be in error to assume that bichordality inevitably invites an association with ambivalence. It is how the music and story combine that brings credence to the dramatic effectiveness of this technique. It is also a question of how this technique is used compositionally. In these* measures, the integrity of C and D is made clear by a simultaneous prolongation of both harmonies, and the effect is somewhat unstable—exactly what Friedhofer needed.]

Before getting out of the cab, Homer makes a feeble, last-minute attempt to postpone the homecoming by suggesting that they all go to Butch's for a couple of beers. Al, seeing through Homer's apprehension, says firmly, "You're home now, kid." Homer slowly says good-bye and climbs out of the cab. Friedhofer underlines this action by a change of key to A major and a change of texture, wherein the bass line now moves in a note-to-note rhythm with the theme (measures 1–5). (See Ex. IV.6.)

Note that an "overlap" is indicated in measure 168 of Ex. IV.6. This is for recording purposes only, and it means that the music from that point on is to be recorded on a separate take and spliced there. It is a valuable recording technique, as it allows the orchestra to concentrate on one segment at a time. Generally, the longer the cue the more important this procedure becomes.

Ex. IV.6.                    *Best Years of Our Lives*

## Arrival at Homer's House

Hugo Friedhofer

Homer's little sister is the first to see him standing in front of the house. Musical flourishes in the flutes and violins over an E pedal accentuate her excitement as she runs to tell their parents and Wilma (Homer's girlfriend). The passage culminates at measure 16 when the sister runs into Homer's arms. [*Here, horns and clarinets are given a lyrical statement of the minor third idea referred to as* x, *over a* $I_4^6$–$ii_2^4$–$V^7$–$V_2^4$ *of IV–IV$^7$ progression (measures 16–19). As the parents run to hug him, Friedhofer restates the "Neighbors" theme using root position ninth chords (measures 19–22) and ends on a second inversion of the tonic to avoid a sense of closure.*] Wilma is seen approaching, and Homer is painfully unsure about what will happen next. (See Ex. IV.7.)

Ex. IV.7.                          *The Best Years of Our Lives*

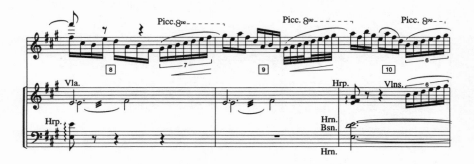

Only one additional theme is brought in at this point, and appropriately enough, it is the theme for the girlfriend, Wilma (measures 23–28). Unlike the *Best Years* and "Boone City" themes, which are associated with a collective point of view, Wilma's theme identifies with the personal. It seems tailored to her. The theme is a relatively straightforward but touching musical idea that moves in almost constant eighth-note motion, centering on the pitches of an A-major triad. It is brought to an end as Wilma embraces Homer. Homer, as though frozen to the spot, arms at his sides, cannot allow himself to respond to her, and the music repeats a concluding fragment of Wilma's theme, first in the middle register and then an octave lower in the horn part (measures 27–28).

A close-up shows Homer's consternation, and Friedhofer alludes to the *Best Years* theme in C$\sharp$ minor for this, connecting the collective tragedies of war with Homer's personal tragedy (measure 29). When the father reaches for Homer's duffel bag, Homer insists on carrying it himself. Everybody sees Homer's artificial hands, and his mother, overcome, begins to sob. It is a moment of such extreme emotion that no musical accent is required. Instead, Friedhofer brings the entire cue to an end with fragments of the *Best Years* theme over a C$\sharp$ pedal. This remarkable sequence ends as Homer and his family enter the house. (See Ex. IV.8.)

Ex. IV.8.   *The Best Years of Our Lives*

**Hugo Friedhofer**

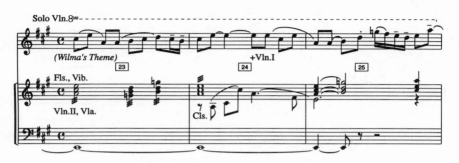

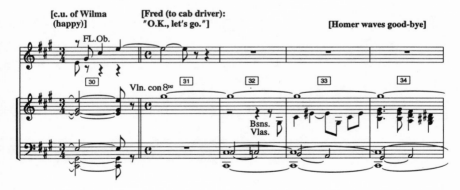

*(continued)*

(continued)

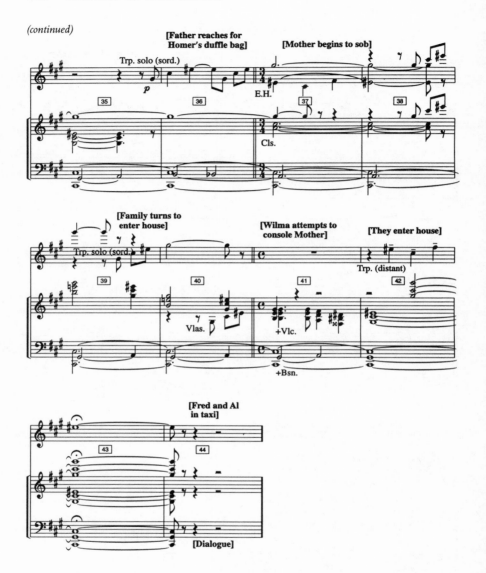

## *Laura:* Apartment Scene

The score for *Laura* (1944) was written by David Raksin just a few years before *The Best Years of Our Lives,* and, like *Best Years,* it has become a classic in film music. In this case, however, the music is additionally known for the theme, which has itself become a classic. At last count, "Laura" had been recorded by more than four hundred performers, ranking second only to "Stardust." Cole Porter once said that of all the songs written by others, he would most liked to have written "Laura."

Raksin wrote the *Laura* theme before tackling the actual score for the film. While this may not sound unusual, there were, at the time, extenuating circumstances. Two things happened to set the wheels in motion: Raksin liked the picture immediately, but at a meeting in Darryl Zanuck's projection room, he heard the disheartening news that Zanuck intended to shorten the central Apartment Scene. In this scene, Mark, the detective, is alone in Laura's apartment. Ostensibly conducting a routine police investigation, he is visibly moved by Laura's portrait, which hangs on the wall. Raksin protested: "If you cut that scene, nobody will understand that the detective is [falling] in love with Laura." Knowing full well that one did not challenge Zanuck's judgment lightly, Raksin, nevertheless, persisted: "This is one of those scenes in which music could tip the balance—tell the audience how the man feels. And if it doesn't work you can still trim the sequence." Later, Raksin was warned by an associate: "I hope you realize what you've done. From now on, when that scene doesn't work, it's your fault!"[1]

As if this weren't enough to pressure a young film composer (he was barely into his thirties at the time), Raksin met with producer-director Otto Preminger a few days later and discovered Preminger's intention to use Duke Ellington's "Sophisticated Lady" as the theme. Raksin remembers saying: "Much as I admired the tune and its urbane composer, I thought it wrong for the film because of the accretion of ideas and associations that a song already so well known would evoke in the audience." Preminger's response was sobering enough. He said, "All right—today is Friday. If you can come in with something we like by Monday, okay. Otherwise we use 'Sophisticated Lady'!"[2]

While Raksin had been working in movies for several years and had plenty of experience dealing with deadlines, it is easy to imagine the paralyzing effect of this ultimatum. Nevertheless, after an emotionally charged, anxiety-ridden weekend during which he wrote dozens of melodies and tore most of them up, the *Laura* theme was born on Sunday night and approved the next day.

Let's look first at some aspects of the theme, which Raksin used to great advantage when adapting it to the needs of the dramatic score, and then, secondly, at the music for the Apartment Scene in its entirety. The manner in which the emotional curve and story line are brought out by the music points up the inspired nature of this cue.

*Thematic Interruption and Truncation*

One of the most striking structural aspects of the *Laura* theme is the descending step progression in the melodic line. [*On the surface, the progression appears as a chromatic chain moving by half steps. The half steps can be viewed or heard as chromatic passing tones connecting diatonic scale steps.*] (See Ex. IV.9.)

The compelling nature of this scalar descent is so strong that an interruption along the way—when suddenly the tune is not allowed to continue—will create a feeling of momentary deliberation and expectation. For instance, imagine stopping at the end of the fourth measure and holding the last note. The ear immediately picks up on a need to continue, and the effect is one of anticipation. We will see how this effect is put to dramatic use early in the Apartment Scene.

Raksin also draws upon a truncated version of the first phrase that allows the line to continue to descend without pause. This is accomplished by eliminating measures 3 and 4 altogether. The effect is one of heightened intensity, which again fulfills dramatic functions in the sequence. (See Ex. IV.9.)

Ex. IV.9.                                    *Laura*

**David Raksin**

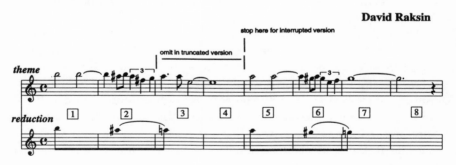

*Tonal Structure*

The tonal structure of the *Laura* theme is of particular interest and not easily analyzed. There are several issues involved, not the least of which is the question of key. Some feel that the piece is in G and ends in the subdominant. Raksin himself is of this opinion. Others contend that C major is the overriding tonality. In either case, most will agree that from the outset of the piece, the ultimate harmonic destination is not readily known. [*The* *overall progression is in constant motion; never does the music hover over a single given tonic. Yet, if regarded on a deeper level, the harmonic and linear structures take on a certain shape that invites an answer, no matter how tentative, to the question of key. The first half of the theme consists of a series of tonicizations by means of ii–V–I progressions in G, F, and E$^b$ respectively, thus challenging G as a key center. An implied return to G in the last four measures of the first ending—the expected G chord in measure 15 is avoided in order to prepare for the repeat—tends to refocus attention on G. Significantly, this implication is somewhat confirmed in the opening measures of the repeat, where G is reinstated. (See Ex. IV.10a, b.)*

*[Richmond Browne, a professor at the University of Michigan, suggests there is a persuasive argument for the G-major tonality conditioned by the way the tune "wraps around not only to the repeat but to the next chorus, i.e., always back to G as tonic." However, Browne feels that in actuality, a stronger case can be made for C major, where "G is an extended V until the end." Working from an analytical sketch of his, I have arrived at a reduction that may demonstrate this point of view. In this reduction, the background level G is prolonged in the bass line until the beginning of the second half. From that point on, it "concatenates" more convincingly as dominant in C major. (See Ex. IV.10b.)*

*[The melodic line echoes the same structural process as the bass. In the first half, on a middle-ground level, it touches upon a 3 2 1 in G, moves through F to E$^b$, and by means of an octave transference to the upper E$^b$ lands on the definitive fifth, D. In the second half, the top line continues beyond the G to F, and finally to a 3 2 1 in C major. A crucial turn occurs on the E$^b$ preceding the final scale-wise descent. In my view, the E$^b$ functions as an appoggiatura to the E.]*

There are three reasons I mention the above analytical observations: One has to do with the music–compositional approach for the entire film. The score, in short, is basically monothematic. Virtually every cue, including most of the source music, makes reference to the *Laura* theme. To my knowledge, this was the first score for a major picture that was based almost exclusively on a single melody—an almost unheard-of approach at that time. In addition, there is something about the *Laura* theme that is uniquely capable of carrying this load. Aside from the obvious, which is that the theme captured an essential aspect of the characters involved (and of Laura in particular), its structural curve allowed for and, in fact, encouraged repetition. Not only was the theme right for the film (and when things are right, repetition is welcomed), but also the linear-structural element of the theme happily "wraps around" to successive statements.

Secondly, the movement of the overall harmonic progression admits more readily to a touchstone effect, in which a need to continue almost always exists. Further, the melody itself presses on throughout its entirety.

Ex. IV.10a.                    *Laura*

**Laura Theme**

**David Raksin**

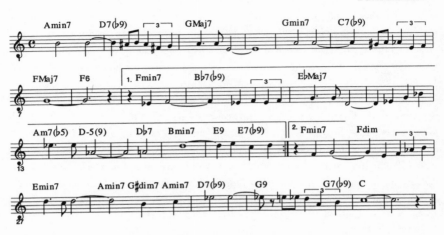

Ex. IV.10b.                    *Laura*

**David Raksin**

It is anything but predictable, and because of this, its use within a dramatic context becomes all the more viable.

Lastly, there is the question of the final cadence. Raksin says that when he was writing the score he "more or less unconsciously hit upon the idea of keeping the tune from coming to a rest," that is, ending before he really meant to do so. Raksin continues, "The fact that this device of *resolutus-interruptus* is consistent even to the end may be attributable to the nature of the final scene in which I think the music is saying farewell to Laura."[3] [*This is compatible with the notion of an extended V, which keeps the final linear and harmonic resolution in reserve until the very end of the film.*]

## The Apartment Scene

At this point we can turn to an analysis of the Apartment sequence. Throughout this scene, it is understood that Laura (Gene Tierney) has been murdered, and it is only at the end of the scene that we discover she is alive. Mark (Dana Andrews), the investigating detective, goes to Laura's apartment to look for clues. It is nighttime, and the music is brought in as he approaches the building. Muted brass in ascending major triads over a B♭ pedal introduce an atmosphere of uncertainty as he talks to the detective stationed at the door and then enters the building. [*Notice that the triads progress by minor thirds; their identity within any particular key is thus canceled out.*] (See Ex. IV.11.)

Ex. IV.11.                          *Laura*

## Apartment Scene

*Part I*                                              **David Raksin**

[Mark approaches in rain ]

*(continued)*

(continued)

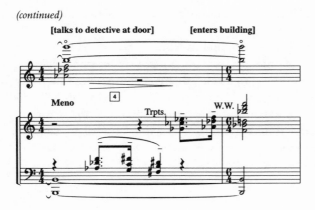

In the next shot, Mark enters the darkened apartment, turns on the lights, and walks into the front room. Descending triads in parallel motion played by woodwinds follow him as he moves toward, then gazes at, Laura's portrait. Raksin particularizes the moment by assigning a fragment of the theme to the alto flute and bassoon (measure 8), then breaks it off when Mark turns from the portrait to remove his coat. To reiterate, an interruption of this sort can heighten our expectation for a resumption of the line, and in the process can also raise questions about the dramatic situation. While this process may operate for us on an unconscious level—our attention is on the film, after all—it is important to remember that the theme has been stated over and over again in the film thus far, and the Apartment Scene takes place in reel 5. We're familiar with the theme and the different ways it has been handled by now. In any case, the fragment makes a dramatic statement, and by association with the portrait on the screen, it says something about Laura and the impression her image makes on the detective. (See Ex. IV.12.)

In a thinly disguised effort to put the portrait's effect behind him and to get on with his job, Mark loosens his tie and walks purposefully to the next room. The music maintains the same feeling of uncertainty introduced at the beginning of the cue. Indeed, the rhythm of the ascending line in the bass clarinet (measure 12) is taken from the ascending brass chord idea in the opening. Raksin builds on this feeling by inserting a slight accent in the muted brass (measure 15) as Mark turns on the lights in the connecting room. Note how this accent is repeated in measures 16 and 17, echoing the initial accent and keeping the effect alive.

Sitting at Laura's desk, Mark takes some letters and a diary out of the drawer and casually tosses them on the desktop. An important shift in in-

Ex. IV.12.    *Laura*

## Apartment Scene

**David Raksin**

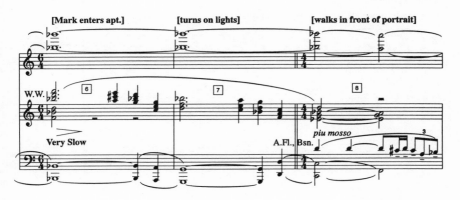

tensity takes place in the score. As Mark mulls over the letters, the music suddenly takes off in an abridged or truncated version, in diminution, of the first eight measures of the tune. It completely changes the pace of the sequence (measure 20). The interesting thing is that there is nothing on the screen to indicate that something should happen. Raksin explains: "This is a risky thing to do, but I believed that the curve of tension should be rising here, and it was not as visible as it should be. I wanted to make the point that this pragmatic man, the detective, was growing uncomfortable with

Ex. IV.13. *Laura*

## Apartment Scene

David Raksin

his feelings about the girl in the portrait, the dead girl, which is hardly the most practical thing that can happen to a guy."[4]

## Negative Accent

His frustration rising, Mark stubs out his cigarette (measure 23). Raksin felt that "this was not a very big action, but the way he did it says something. However, it didn't say it clearly enough. Therefore, the music rises somewhat [measures 20–23], trying not to overdo it, and instead of doing the usual thing of providing some kind of an accent, it does just the opposite, a negative accent. When he stubs out the cigarette, the music suddenly gets very soft to prepare for another long rise."[5] (See Ex. IV.13.)

## Parallel Situation

A parallel situation emerges at this point in the scene. Where a moment ago the detective had walked into Laura's study and turned on the lights, he now walks into her bedroom and does the same. Raksin plays on the similarity of these two situations by bringing back the same music—the ascending bass clarinet line and a muted brass chord to accentuate the lit room. However, because of the developing dramatic curve, Raksin, from measure 30 on, takes up a different line of musical thought. As Mark walks to Laura's dresser, picks a filmy handkerchief from the drawer, unstops a vial of perfume to smell the fragrance, then replaces the stopper, Raksin reintroduces the descending triadic idea in the winds (measure 30) that was

Ex. IV.14.                                    *Laura*

## Apartment Scene

David Raksin

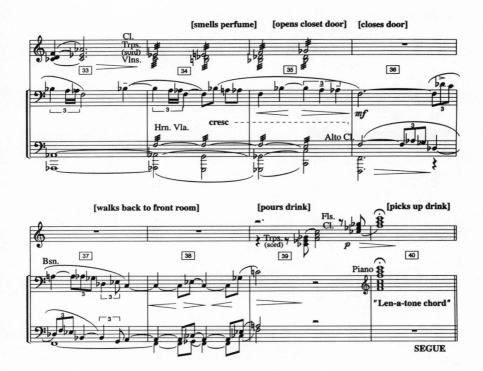

used at the beginning of the scene, when the detective entered the apartment (measures 6–7). This prepares for a second, quiet statement of the interrupted version of the theme (measures 32–33). Raksin could have pointed up the handkerchief and the perfume, but doing so would have resulted in too many accents. Instead, reference to the theme here does more to refocus our attention on the detective's real feelings.

Subsequently, Mark goes to the closet and finds a negligée. Here again, as he closes the closet door, the music almost vanishes, providing a negative accent (measure 36). The accent here says that, from the detective's point of view, things have gone too far. He shuts the closet door, walks back to the front room, and pours himself a drink. (See Ex. IV.14.)

### Thematic Reference

Thus far in the sequence, fragments of the theme are brought in at critical points to suggest that the detective is unconsciously beginning to feel drawn to Laura: when he stands before her portrait, when he discovers her letters

Ex. IV.15.                                        *Laura*

## Apartment Scene

*Part Ia*                                                    **David Raksin**

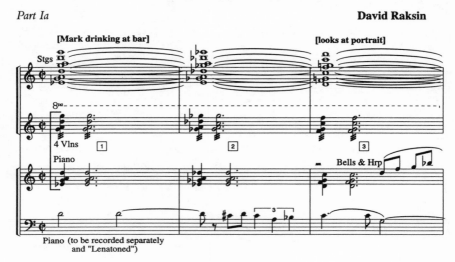

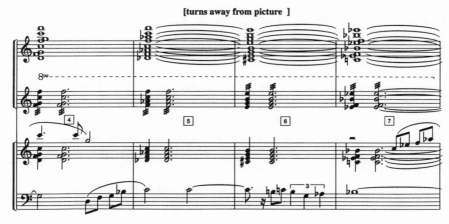

and diary, and when he picks her handkerchief out of the drawer. This kind of selective thematic reference is, of course, a useful technique in film music when there is a need to bring out a dramatic thread.

Part I of the score segues to Part Ia. This is a twenty-seven-second continuation of the cue that consists almost entirely of the first eight measures of the theme. The music builds on what had only been hinted at before—

the detective's vulnerability in this situation. Standing in the front room, the detective takes a gulp of his drink and walks to the portrait to take a closer look. He seems to have momentarily dropped his guard. The music plays no small role in establishing this. At some point, the detective snaps out of his reverie and goes to the phone to check with the other detective stationed in the basement of the building. [*Notice how easily Raksin wraps up the cue, in measures 8–10, by avoiding an expected resolution to G-minor harmony and moving instead to a second inversion of a dominant of F, with an added ninth and augmented eleventh. It is a highly crafted and succinct way of taking the music out without imposing the feeling of a complete close.*] (See Ex. IV.15.)

In measure 1 of Part Ia, there is a notation that the piano part is to be recorded separately and that this track is to be "Len-a-toned." Raksin knew that if the capstan of a playback deck was milled into an oval shape, there would be a distinct, waver-like distortion in the sound. After some experimentation with different-sized oval shapes, and assisted by Harry Leonard (after whom the device was later named), Raksin arrived at a configuration that produced only a slight waver in the playback—the effect he wanted. The result proved to be absolutely appropriate for this scene, which shows Mark's increasing discomfort with his own emotions.

After the phone call, Mark is interrupted by an unexpected visitor, Waldo (Clifton Webb), who enters and provokes an argumentative conversation. Waldo, a fast-talking sophisticate, journalist, and radio commentator, knew Laura well. He perceives Mark's inordinate interest in the case and says pompously, "You better be careful, you'll end up in a psychiatric ward. I don't think they ever had a patient who fell in love with a corpse." When Waldo leaves, the music is brought back as the camera stops on a close-up of the detective.

One single "Len-a-toned" chord by the piano connects the beginning of Part II with the end of Part Ia. In Part II, the chords in measures 1 and 7 were recorded in the following manner. The pianist struck the chord while the microphones were turned off. A beat later, the microphones were turned on, catching only the sustained and decay characteristics of the sound. What is recorded, then, is the interplay of the partials without the attack and initial drop. This, treated by the "Len-a-toned" device, created a special echoing sound that connected Part Ia with Part II. Despite the interruption of several minutes of dialogue, the quality of the music (including the specialness of the wavering sound), and the closeness with which it identifies with the dramatic situation, readily creates an immediacy of association with the earlier section of the cue.

Part II begins with a close-up of Mark's face and, four seconds later, dissolves to a medium shot of Mark standing alone at the buffet, struggling for self-control as he pours himself another drink. On the dissolve, Raksin reintroduces the truncated form of the theme, which, as earlier in the sequence (when Mark had been sitting at Laura's desk), suddenly energizes the moment. In so doing, the music both rebounds off Waldo's acerbic comments and refocuses our attention on Mark's inner conflict.

Mark turns from the buffet, walks across the room toward the portrait, and sinks into an easy chair. His stride is in near synchronization with the musical pulse. Whether Raksin intended this, or whether it was decided in the editing, the effect works in a subtle way, bringing out Mark's final, determined effort to cope with the situation. (See Ex. IV.16.)

A *rallentando* (a gradual slowing up of the tempo) in the music leads to a sustained chord (measures 7–8) as Mark settles into the chair. What follows brings the sequence to an end, simply and conclusively. Exhausted, the detective gazes into space, looks again at the portrait, and falls asleep. The second half of the *Laura* theme is brought in for this. However, this time the theme is kept intact, with no interruptions. It carries the relatively long shot (measures 9–23). Significantly, the theme ends on the penultimate harmony—the final resolution to the tonic is avoided—as the camera dollies back and the real-life Laura is seen entering the apartment. She has been on vacation and has no idea she is presumed dead. By avoiding a resolution to the tonic, Raksin creates a sense of anticipation that, considering Laura's entrance, is appropriate. The camera motion to Laura is highlighted by a secondary accent in the piano part (measure 22). Here and

Ex. IV.16.                          *Laura*

## Apartment Scene

*Part II*                                                          **David Raksin**

throughout Part II, the chords were originally recorded on two tracks, both
"Len-a-toned," and alternated in the final mix so as to create a sense of
"phasing." (See Ex. IV.17.)

The Apartment Scene in *Laura* is well known to many film composers.
It is often referred to as a model of film composing, and it is one of the
most memorable music cues that I know.

Ex. IV.17.                              *Laura*

## Apartment Scene

David Raksin

## *East of Eden:* Climactic Scene

In the last chapter, we dealt with the question of release points within a dramatic line. I have found it useful on occasion to make a distinction between a point of release and what might be considered the climactic moment of a story. As has been suggested, the point of release occurs when things come together, where a solution has been found. For me, the climax of a story is somewhat different. It is where the conflict is completely out

[He looks at portrait]

[Mark falls asleep]    [Camera dollies back]                    [Laura
                                                                enters]

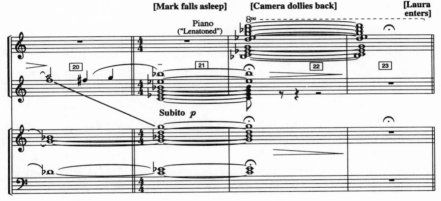

in the open and there is no apparent solution. Generally, the climax of a film requires music to bring out the explosive potential of the moment and to build on elements central to the dramatic line. A perfect example of this occurs toward the end of the monumental score for *East of Eden*.

In what may be considered the climactic scene of *Eden*, Cal (James Dean) drags his brother, Aaron, to a nearby bordello to introduce him to the establishment's owner/madam—their mother—whom Aaron has thought to be dead. The sequence strips the main characters of any lingering pretensions and exposes their raw inner fears and predilections.

## Expressionistic Style

The score, written by Leonard Rosenman, contains many significant aspects, not the least of which is the musical language employed for the more intense scenes of the film. The language is highly chromatic and expressionistic, which in 1955 was considered to be relatively unorthodox in film music. When Rosenman brought this style to film, many were excited about how well this direction pointed up the story.

Numerous factors entered in: Rosenman's own concert music style at the time, which reflected his studies with Arnold Schoenberg and Roger Sessions; the nature of the *Eden* film, which, because of its psychological content, lent itself to an intensified musical treatment; and, perhaps equally important, the openness of its director, Elia Kazan, to a different musical approach. To be exact, the expressionistic musical style had found its way into isolated moments of many film scores before *Eden,* including scores by Hanns Eisler, David Raksin, and others. Still, I believe that it is in *Eden* and in *Cobweb* (1955), written soon after, that this style came into full view.

### The Situation

It is important to know what immediately precedes the climactic sequence in question: Cal has just suffered what he feels is the ultimate rejection from his father. After having laboriously raised beans to earn money, which he offers his father as a birthday present, the father refuses the gift, saying he won't benefit from something that had cost the lives of young men. Because of World War I, Cal's bean crop sold at a great profit. Cal had thought that his action would win his father's affection and respect. Instead, the father demands that Cal try to be more like his brother, Aaron, the son he had always favored. The rejection of the gift brings Cal to the breaking point, and, sobbing, he runs out of the house.

In the scene that begins the climactic sequence, Cal, in the backyard, has disappeared behind a tree. It is nighttime. No music as yet. Abra, Aaron's girlfriend, runs after Cal to console him, and Aaron follows her. Aaron, who is something of a weak character, calls Cal "bad and vicious" and demands that Cal stay away from Abra. Silence. The music begins at the precise moment that Cal moves out from behind the tree toward Aaron.

Rosenman opens the cue with a repeated chord idea followed by an arpeggiated figure in the muted brass. As the brass "hold" on the accumulated notes, the repeated chord idea is restated. The nature of the complex harmonies and the thudding chordal figure instantly infuse the scene with a sense of foreboding. Cal says his first line: "You want to go some place with me, Aaron?" The music gives warning that the time for confrontation has come. (See Ex. IV.18.)

Ex. IV.18.                              *East of Eden*

**Leonard Rosenman**

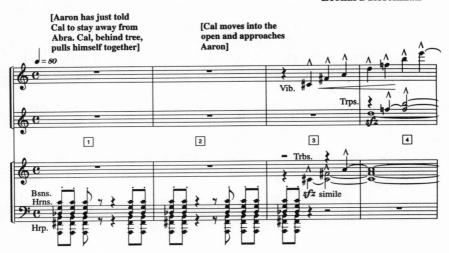

*Lighting*

Significantly, eighteen seconds pass before Cal's first line—a formidable length of time on film unless, of course, there is something there to carry the shot. Here, Cal's anguish is in the forefront. His sudden silence and slow, deliberate movement out from behind the tree have treacherous implications. Would this be sufficient to rule out the need for music? I don't think so. An important consideration—the lighting—must be taken into account. The shot, by necessity, is low-lit, and the characters as well as their facial expressions are barely discernible. Cal's change of attitude, from frustration to deep-set anger—basic to the whole sequence—is not as clear perhaps as it should be. Thus, it falls to the music to bring this out.

*Motivic Approach*

From the outset, the music has a repeated chord pattern that is given momentum by rhythmically additive means. (See Ex. IV.19.)

Ex. IV.19.                              *East of Eden*

[*The chord itself has a questioning, ambivalent quality that can be analyzed only in the context of how it is followed. For instance, the top note of the chord, C, clearly gives way to the C# in measure 3, the beginning pitch of the arpeggiated figure. The remaining notes of the chord are treated in a much more complex manner. Notice that the pitches of an F#-minor triad are embedded in the chord and that these pitches are restated in the opening of the arpeggiation. This connection, subtly stated by means of octave transferral, suggests an affirmation of the F#-minor triad, in which case the remaining notes of the chord can then be heard as appoggiaturas, subtly resolved in the arpeggiation. (See Ex. IV.20.)*]

[*The passage becomes more complex as linear and harmonic relationships mentioned above are detached from their origins and redirected. In measure 5, for instance, the upper four notes of the repeated chord have been transposed up a step while the lower two notes, A and F#, are preserved. The effect is that of a wedge being driven into the chord complex itself, forcing one segment (x) away from its initial position, creating an auxiliary function (y) and an expectation for a return (x), which takes place in measure 8. (See Ex. IV.21.)*]

The chord returns many times throughout the sequence and becomes a key element in preparation for the climactic ending. Technically, it func-

Ex. IV.20.                      *East of Eden*

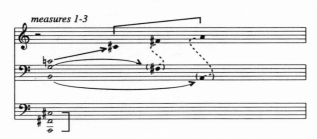

Ex. IV.21.                      *East of Eden*

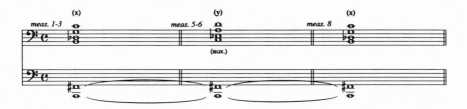

tions as a kind of pedal point, and as a source from which pitches in the upper register are derived. More important, the repeated chord idea is in dramatic contrast to a brief melodic line introduced in measure 7. This melodic material brings out a momentary inner feeling of reflection not observable on-screen. Combined with the chordal idea, it helps force the issue and elicit the feeling of resolve implicit in Cal's behavior.

[*In measure 8 the violin line, which has been holding a high B (taken from the sustained brass chord), suddenly rebounds off Cal's first line. This melodic idea, taken from an earlier cue, is the source of successive variant statements throughout the first half of the sequence. (See Ex. IV.22.)*]

At this point (measure 9), Rosenman brings back the repeated chordal figure that sets up Cal's next line: "I got something to show you." The word "something" is a euphemism, of course, because what Cal has in mind will take Aaron's world apart. [*This line is accompanied by a variant of Cal's five-note motive (discussed in Chapter 2 in relation to the opening scene of the film), followed by a sixteenth-note triplet idea stated by the bass clarinet, harp, and piano (measure 11). This sixteenth-note motive provides an additional impetus to Cal's action and his next words.*] Leaping up alongside a tree,

Ex. IV.22.                                    *East of Eden*

**Leonard Rosenman**

Cal says, "Maybe our mother didn't die and go to heaven after all, Aaron."
A complex arpeggiated dyadic figure in the harp sustains the thought
(measure 13) and prepares for Cal's next line, a blockbuster: "Maybe she's
alive someplace." (See Ex. IV.23.)

*Musical Intensity and Sudden Dialogue*

For the rest of this scene (up to the dissolve to the bordello), Cal recounts
an instance pointing out their mother's "goodness"—a quality with which
Aaron himself identifies—and Cal's "badness." This sudden rush of dia-

Ex. IV.23.                                    *East of Eden*

**Leonard Rosenman**

logue created a problem for the music, and it is one that occurs quite frequently in film scoring. Rosenman had to back off somewhat to allow space
for the dialogue and still maintain the already established level of intensity.
Any drop in intensity here would compromise the evolving climactic arch
of the entire sequence. Rosenman solved the problem discreetly, drawing
on established material.

Beginning with measure 17, Rosenman recalls the repeated chord motive to punctuate Cal's recollections of his and Aaron's childhood stories.
Strings and muted horns hold on a chord as Cal begins talking hurriedly.
In measure 20, the repeated chord idea is stated once again, but this time
by muted brass in the middle register, which lightens the musical texture.
The next five measures (measures 21–25) consist mainly of a lyrical extension in the violins (vaguely reminiscent of Cal's five-note motive, discussed
in Chapter 2). The music is more transparent here than in preceding measures, and it is in this manner that Rosenman is able to provide textural
space for the dialogue. This passage, incidentally, is accompanied by a series
of rising fourth chords in the bassoons and clarinets functioning as a kind of
pervasive chorale which, as Rosenman suggests, perpetuates the primitive,
religious idea that the mother has gone to heaven.

There remains, however, the question of intensity and how it is maintained. Two things should be noted in this regard. First, the violin line itself
(measures 21–25): notice that it consists of several leaps, large and small,
encompassing nearly a two-octave range. A high level of expressivity is thus
contained within the line, which allows for a continuation of the intensity
level. Secondly, Rosenman has said that he often leaves "holes" in the mu-

sic for the voice to be "utilized as a sort of speaking instrument."[6] In this sequence, the rhythmic interaction between the dialogue and the music becomes a significant resource in the effort to create a sense of concentrated space for both media.

Later, when Cal asks, "Can you look at the truth?" Rosenman brings back the sixteenth-note triplet and repeated chord ideas as a means of punctuation (measure 27). The scene ends with a widespread chord consisting of all notes of the chromatic scale (except D), as Cal urges Aaron forward. This sonority, which demands resolution, prepares for the cut to the next section. (See Ex. IV.24.)

As has been mentioned, the problem of maintaining musical intensity when there is a sudden rush of dialogue is a common one for film composers. It originates with the way scenes are often constructed on film. A critical sequence can, and often does, begin with establishing shots with little or no dialogue. Close-ups and cuts from one angle are used to introduce the scene. However, music is often required to heighten what is suggested at the outset, when meanings and levels of emotion are not clear enough. Assuming for the moment that music is needed for the rest of the sequence, a problem arises when the dialogue or action suddenly takes off. This forces the music to shift gears or to make space for the dialogue without any loss of intensity. In this case, a musical solution must be found. I have seen many pictures in which inattention to this detail has been detrimental to the expressivity of the scene and its overall dramatic shape.

Ex. IV.24.                              *East of Eden*

**Leonard Rosenman**

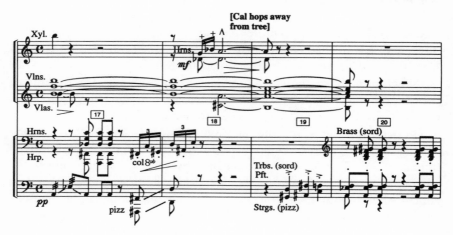

## Motivic Ideas and Subsequent Dramatic Needs

Given the musical material at hand, Rosenman is perfectly positioned to score the rest of the scene up to the climactic end. Each motive serves in the interest of subsequent needs.

On the dissolve to the hallway in the bordello, Rosenman brings back the repeated chord figure, which is doubly punctuated in the strings by means of thirty-second notes (measure 33). The effect is extremely forceful and prepares for what follows in the next measure (34). Winds and trumpets in unison are given Cal's five-note motive, which has been used throughout the film in association with Cal's scenes with or about his

*(continued)*

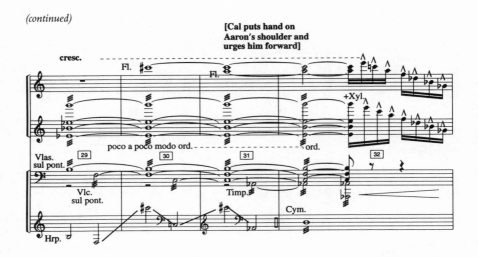

mother, Kate. By this scene, in reel 13, the motive has acquired a meaning and a power that could only have been developed and realized over time.

A variant of the five-note motive is stated vigorously by three horns (measure 37), and this corresponds to the moment where the camera tightens on Cal and Aaron approaching their mother's doorway. The repeated chord motive quickly picks up on the muscular quality of the action. As the two brothers finally stand in front of the door, Rosenman brings back the sixteenth-note triplet figure that swoops upward through a chain of tritone-related intervals and leads emphatically to a high B♭, when Cal opens the door and walks in. (See Ex. IV.25.)

[*One additional musical idea enters at measure 36, and this is first stated by the trombones. Notice that the outer voices of this chordal progression form the intervals of a perfect fifth, an augmented fifth, and then a major seventh. Though the idea was introduced several reels before, it is used here in association with Cal's ominous intentions and tends to corroborate the*

Ex. IV.25.                    *East of Eden*

**Leonard Rosenman**

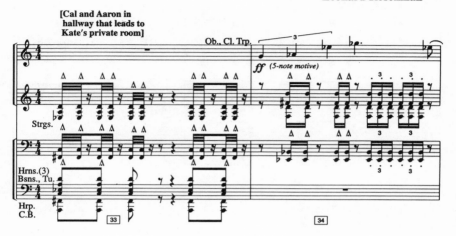

*(continued)*

*(continued)*

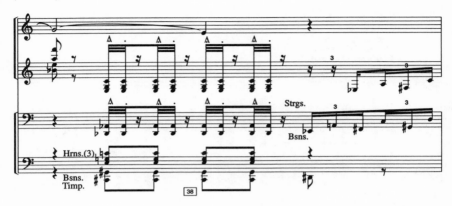

*slow, deliberate style of his delivery. Note also how, in terms of voice leading, it prepares for a harmonic variant of the repeated note idea. (See Ex. IV.26.)]*

Their mother, Kate, who has been dozing, wakes and sees Cal before her. Smiling pathetically and revealing her vulnerability for the first time in the film, she is visibly uneasy and emotionally stirred. The music here plays on these sensibilities, on the nature of the dramatic situation itself, and, more particularly, on the psychological pacing of events. Muted brass in half notes (measures 42–43) "feel" their way through a short progression, followed by a fragment of the five-note motive in augmentation, which coincides with a close-up of Kate (in measure 44). The falling minor

Ex. IV.26.                         *East of Eden*

third of the motive, which has an unmistakable pleading quality, is reiterated by the piccolo, celesta, flute, and harp in the upper register (measure 45).

A return of the repeated chord idea (measure 47) prepares for a cut to Cal. As he turns to Aaron, Rosenman makes one final, almost heartrending statement with the five-note motive (oboe and clarinet in unison, measure 48). But suddenly the music takes off, preparing for the shot of Aaron's appearance in the doorway (measures 49–50). To allow for and absorb Aaron's incredulous reaction, the brass sustain an arpeggiated chord (an effective stylistic trait in Rosenman's music) consisting of superimposed augmented triads; abruptly, this is replaced by strings alone as Cal introduces Aaron to their mother (measures 52–56).

At this point, the agonizing silence in the room (not in the score) is taken over by a chordal progression consisting of descending minor triads over a D pedal (horns and pizzicato strings, measures 57–59). Kate, dread in her face, looks on. Finally, Cal says, "Aaron, say hello to your mother." The line is a cue for the final build-up to the climactic breaking point of the entire sequence. A gradually unfolding chromatic chordal complex quietly reverberates throughout the string section, joined, significantly, by statements in the woodwinds of the falling minor third idea taken from the five-note motive (measures 60–64). Cal turns to leave but turns back and shouts: "Say hello to your mother, Aaron!" [*The major-seventh dyad in the trumpets, C and B (measure 65), punctuates this release of anger as he pushes Aaron toward their mother and the two fall back onto the sofa. The trumpets hold on the dyad as the trombones glissando to a low C♯, forming a tritone with a high G in woodwinds and strings.*] The music is cut as Cal slams the door, leaving Kate and Aaron alone in the room. (See Ex. IV.27.)

*Source Music as Climactic Aftermath*

One would think the sequence has ended at this point. But Rosenman goes one step further: As a climactic aftermath, he cuts to source music from the barroom as Cal runs down the hallway and through the bar. The pianist is playing an up-tempo version of "Smiles" to a crowd of drunken customers who, after all, have no clue as to what has occurred in the back room. The effect? Stunning. By means of total contrast in spirit and meaning, this music breaks open the whole dramatic line and renders the memory of what has just happened even more emphatic. It also conspires with Cal's sense of unrestrained relief, resolve, and subsequent action.

A parenthetical note: The pianist in this final shot is Rosenman himself. Though perhaps only friends of his will recognize him, it is a nice touch. I can think of only one other instance in film where the composer is shown. In Alfred Hitchcock's *The Man Who Knew Too Much* (1956), Bernard Herrmann conducts a symphony orchestra during an extended sequence in which a murder plot simultaneously unfolds in the concert hall.

*Within the Context of the Film*

Given the two scenes—the backyard and the bordello—it might have been considered possible to keep the music in reserve for the bordello scene, where most of the action takes place and where the highest level of emo-

Ex. IV.27.                              *East of Eden*

**Leonard Rosenman**

*(continued)*

tionality comes into view. In my judgment, however, and clearly in the composer's estimation, this would have amounted not only to a wasted opportunity but also to a tragically minimized impact on the dramatic line. The music enters at the precise moment that the direction of the drama

*(continued)*

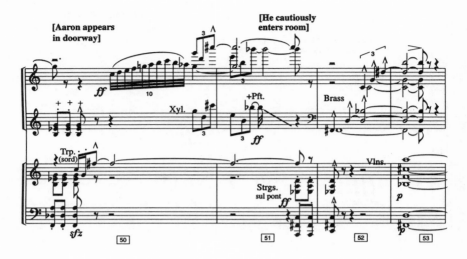

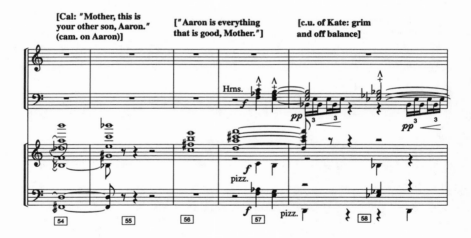

shifts. While this shift is not immediately apparent on the screen, the introduction of music at that point makes it apparent. Furthermore, it is a credit
to Rosenman's choice of musical style and development of material that he
was able to create a deep sense of what brings both of the scenes together
and still build to the horrendous moment at the very end. The sequence is
three minutes and nineteen seconds long. Given the context of the film,
which lasts more than two hours, and a pivotal scene in which so much
has to be put forward on experiential and dramatic levels, these three min–

["Aaron, say hello
to your mother."]

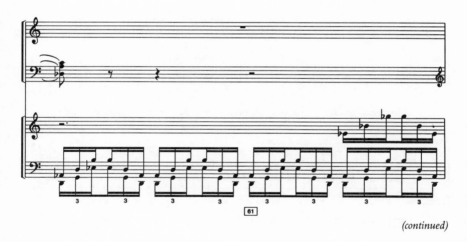

(continued)

utes are well served. Using music for the bordello scene alone would not
have had the same impact. Rosenman's decision to begin with the cut to
the backyard was crucial to the overall effectiveness and meaning of this
extraordinary sequence and, in a broader sense, of the film.

In this chapter and in all preceding chapters, we have placed the emphasis
on where music appeared and with what consequences. Certainly this was
true of the three sequences discussed above. Of almost equal significance,
however, is the question of when or for what reasons music is omitted or
not required. In some places in film, the use of music can be detrimental.
This subject is taken up in the next chapter.

*(continued)*

**[c.u. of Kate (looking disgusted)]**

**[c.u. of Cal and Aaron]**

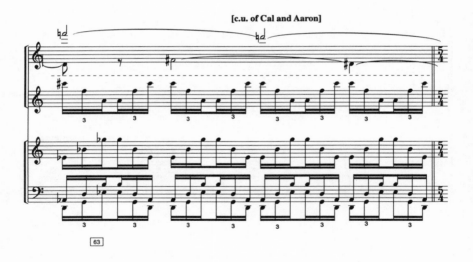

*Chapter Five*

# The Sound and Function of Silence: When Music Is Absent

During the "silent" period, a tradition evolved whereby continuous music (played live) was considered a virtual necessity. At first, music was employed to mask the sound of noisy projectors, which were a terrible distraction. More challenging, however, was the nature of the new medium itself. For one thing, there was the problem of continuity from one image to another. For another, it became obvious that various actions and moods needed amplification of some sort. Music did the trick. Besides which, it was disconcerting to see an actor's lips moving as in mock dialogue, or to see a door slamming without hearing something. Such images viewed in silence created a void. In short, absolute silence—the total absence of both voice and ambient sound—proved to be so deadly to the overall experience that the use of music for film was born.

It was discovered that once music was introduced to a silent film, any let-up or silence was very distracting, as though somebody had suddenly strangled the piano player. It then became standard practice to have continuous, "wall-to-wall" music. But with the advent of "sound" film in the 1930s, attitudes toward the use of music began to change. The presence of ambient sound and dialogue in the film meant that continuous music was no longer necessary. It became apparent that there were moments, and often whole sections, in film that required no music whatsoever, that the omission of music could have a dramatic and unique impact. It also became clear that music preceded by its absence could be more effective and bring far more weight to an event than if it had been present all along.

The extent to which film composers in the 1930s felt pressured by the

205

"silent" film tradition of continuous music is a matter of conjecture, although we can be sure that the tradition had an influence on their approach. The important question, for us, is: Under what generalized circumstances in "sound" film might the exclusion of music be dramatically and cinematographically more effective than its inclusion?

In the broadest context, the use and non-use of music depend on the style, substance, and meaning of a film. For instance, early pictures such as *Captain Blood* (1935) and *Robin Hood* (1938), both of which have outstanding scores by Erich Wolfgang Korngold, were perched right on the edge of operetta style, not as this would apply to the singing style of nineteenth-century Viennese operetta but in terms of dramatic substance. Overall dramatic meanings were distinctly light. Dialogue requiring musical emphasis was either in the interest of a romantic situation or accompanied by action. Such films would naturally give way to a theatrical musical style with continuing music. Far from taking Korngold to task for writing "too much music," as some writers on film music would have it, I think his approach was absolutely appropriate, and that it enhanced rather than compromised the dramatic nature of these films.

In contrast to the above, there were films that addressed matters of deep social concern. One such film was *I Was a Fugitive from a Chain Gang*, a 1930s classic starring Paul Muni. Dramatic (original) music was omitted altogether from this film. The bleakness of the situation was important to the story and to the narrative style in which it was told. No doubt it was decided that this quality would have been canceled out by the sound of a dramatic musical score.

Films of every period raise similar questions. For example, John Williams's extensive musical treatment for *Star Wars* (1977) was compatible with the story and style of the picture. On the other hand, *Save the Tiger* (1973), starring Jack Lemmon, was reminiscent of *Chain Gang*. The main character found himself similarly victimized by a socioeconomic system that forced him into a corner from which it was almost impossible to escape without breaking the law. Music was omitted from this film as well.

There are, in short, circumstances that occur time and time again which suggest the non-use of music. A consideration of some of these can be revealing.

## Matter-of-Fact Dialogue

Probably the most common situation in film that does not require music is when dialogue states the case, particularly the kind of dialogue that presents factual rather than dramatic information. Thus, it may be important to hear every word when someone is offering a sobering analysis of a dilemma, or a summation of what has happened. Even more important, these situations can be complete in themselves; musical emphasis or enhancement is not needed.

*Al Capone*, scored by David Raksin, opens with shots of a barroom in Chicago. No music. An off-camera narrator introduces the story as an "episode in the time of the 1920s" and Al Capone as "a ruthless and cunning criminal." New in town and appearing less than ruthless and cunning at this point, young Capone (Rod Steiger) suddenly enters the bar. The main titles are superimposed over Capone's entrance, and this is where Raksin begins the music. It opens with a highly dissonant gesture which, along with the narrator's words, instantly criminalizes Capone, pinpointing the beginning of the dramatic structural line. The absence of music for the first minute or so of the film not only is respectful of the factual-like narration; it also functions as preparation for the subsequent musical accent.

A special case occurs at the end of *Tora! Tora! Tora!*, where music is included for Admiral Yamamoto's stunning and unforgettable summation. After the Pearl Harbor attack he says, "I fear that all we have done is awaken a sleeping giant and filled him with a terrible resolve." This is indeed a sobering analysis of the situation, but the difference is this: His words possess a poetic ring and have enormous implications. The fact that music, especially main titles music (see Ex. III.10), is used to accompany this line seems especially justifiable. It certainly is effective.

To be sure, dialogue does not rule out the need for music. Many of the examples examined in previous chapters demonstrate the need for music with  dialogue. The climactic sequence from *East of Eden* is a good example. But "under-dialogue" (dialogue accompanied by music) is not the issue here. We are concerned with generalized situations in which music is commonly omitted.

## Psychological Containment

Consider Ingmar Bergman's *Face to Face* (1976), a film with virtually no music. Here there are but two quickly stated chords and the opening measures of Mozart's "Fantasy in C Minor." The chords are introduced at moments of extreme emotion, emphasizing the specific instant. The Mozart excerpt is used only during a scene involving a piano recital and exists as source music. Why so little music? The answer lies in the film's dramatic content. A central intention is to establish that the suppression of anger without release has dangerous psychological consequences. The two major characters repress their anger and become desperately lonely figures. Musical gestures filling out the space of this film would cancel out, or at least be in conflict with, its dramatic intent. The separateness of the characters in their private anguish is more vividly and starkly portrayed without music.

*Compulsion* (1959), another film with a psychological edge, has no music for the entire length of the drama. A theme is used, however, for the beginning and end titles. Directed by Richard Fleischer and starring Orson Welles, the film tells the story of the notorious Leopold and Loeb trial. Fleischer told me he took the finished picture to Lionel Newman for advice on the score, but Newman didn't think the picture needed music— and, after considerable thought, Fleischer arrived at the same conclusion.

*Compulsion,* shot in black and white, casts a dramatic chain of events into sharp relief. In it, unharnessed intellectual brilliance on a college campus gives way to an experimental murder as a test of control under the guise of philosophical reasoning. This sordid act originates with an aberrant form of self-deception, and its enveloping, inescapable consequences are chilling indeed. The story is true, of course, and the acting and direction are totally believable. The film's dramatic pacing is right on the mark. The inclusion of music might have destroyed much of the carefully crafted emergence of senseless impulse—the point of the story. Fleischer, a director of over forty-five films, believes *Compulsion* to be one of his best. I asked him if, at the time of shooting, he had had any indication that history was being made in front of his camera during Welles's long summation at the film's end. He replied that he had and added that even Welles showed signs of nervousness.

The significance of containment within a deep psychological conflict was critical to the meaning and depth of expression in both of these films, and this factor was, in each case, aided by the signal absence of music. Much the same reasoning has worked well for individual sequences. In *One Flew over the Cuckoo's Nest* (1975), music is omitted for most of the scenes that occur in a mental hospital ward. The dialogue takes over as one problem or another is discussed, shouted, or raved about in a zany manner. What emerges with the dialogue is a sense of austerity or emptiness of the human condition as it can be imposed through drugs and therapeutic emasculation. Again, musical silence worked best.

In one outstanding scene, a group therapy session, the patients argue with Nurse Ratched over whether they may watch the World Series on television. Nurse Ratched preempts the session by putting it to a vote but, in an effort to get her way, discounts the Chief's vote and turns down the proposal. Compounding her act of cruelty, she then plays a Mantovani recording over the P.A. system. The patients are forced to listen to her choice of music, which floods the ward and the screen with a soupy kind of string sound, producing a maddening effect. Up to this point, the nature and intensity of the dialogue, coupled with the stark sterility of the ward, abrogated any need for musical emphasis. More important, the absence of music enlarges upon the hideous insult of the sentimentally sweet string music the patients are later forced to endure.

## Acoustic Space

In situations involving the outdoors, the feeling of acoustic space is important to the effect of a scene. For instance, there is a long sequence near the beginning of *Where Eagles Dare* (1968) in which a small group of British and American troops parachute onto a snowbound Alpine field, miles from the German fortress that was their target destination. No music. Ordinarily there would be a strong temptation to use stirring, march-like music to underline the heroism of men facing a difficult mission behind enemy lines, as in a similar scene from *Objective, Burma!* (1945). However, composer Ron Goodwin had something else in mind—an approach that focused more on the dramatic line.

For one thing, the musical silence in this scene allows for an acoustic space in which the chilling remoteness of the field and the absolute secrecy of the maneuver are made real. But just as important is what follows once the parachutists land and silently regroup. One of the men is found dead with a broken neck as a result of strangulation. The music was reserved for this point to draw attention to a key element in the film: Since nobody else is around, someone within their own ranks is evidently attempting to sabotage the operation. Later we find that enemy spies have infiltrated the group, not to mention Allied Command. Again, music kept in reserve for a strategic point is all the more effective when preceded by silence. In this case, the omission of music first draws attention to the majestic quality of the field, and this quality serves, by means of contrast, as a dramatic lead-in to the discovery of the murder itself.

This reminds me of another well-known scene in a field—a field in the American midwest in Alfred Hitchcock's *North by Northwest* (1959). Here again, the absence of music in relation to acoustic space played well, considering the dramatic context and meaning of the scene.

In this scene Cary Grant gets off a bus only to find himself at the edge of a vast and seemingly deserted cornfield. Hitchcock thought it essential to omit music from this sequence. Its absence emphasizes the remoteness of the location and the unreasonableness of Grant's situation. It even helps render more comic the business of the farmer who waits across the road for a bus bound in the opposite direction.

A short while later, a crop-dusting biplane appears, and because "there ain't no crops to dust" it becomes clear that the pilot intends to swoop down on Grant in a life-threatening manner. Still Hitchcock employs no music—the silence of the field and the roar of the biplane's engine is enough. In an interview with François Truffaut, Hitchcock said that he was "not dealing with time, but with space . . . to indicate the various distances that a man had to run for cover and, more than that, to show that there was no cover to run to."[1]   Music might well have negated this feeling of distance by inadvertently providing an aural buffer behind Grant's erratic attempts to escape. The entire sequence, up to the point at which the plane crashes into an oncoming truck, is about seven minutes long and entirely without music.

On a larger scale, there is an almost twenty-minute sequence without music near the beginning of *Pat and Mike* (1952), which takes place on a golf course. The feeling of the outdoors is prevalent in this sequence, and everyone is wrapped up in the tournament and in the players' need for quiet concentration. Musical comment is not required. Katharine Hepburn plays the part of a budding golf and tennis pro, and Spencer Tracy plays the sports promoter. Not until Tracy finally sees Hepburn as a woman rather than just another potential client does composer David Raksin bring in a soft and bluesy tune. The story suddenly moves in another direction in which "concentration" is not the issue, and Raksin's music helps establish this change.

## Moments of Anguish

Sometimes a film sequence will focus upon an instance of personal embarrassment, awkwardness, ineptness, or even anguish. Moments like these often call for a hush on the sound track—while, in effect, the audience winces and hopes the character will be able to get through it all. For instance, when a guest at a formal dinner drops a spoon or spills something, we feel embarrassed for the person and hope the incident will go unnoticed.

Sometimes a minute detail can be accentuated by the omission of music, especially when the shot itself makes the point. In a scene from Hitchcock's *To Catch a Thief* (1955), the wastefulness in the lives of the very rich is poetically revealed and enhanced when a sophisticated breakfast table conversation in a hotel suite overlooking the Côte d'Azur is interrupted by a cutaway to a close-up of a hand grinding out a cigarette into the yolk of a mouth-watering, untouched poached egg. Shots like this require no musical emphasis because they say all that needs to be said.

### When the Situation Carries the Shot

On the other hand, imagine a moment of extreme anguish wherein a person's life is coming apart and this necessitates a confrontation. A really striking example appears in William Wyler's *The Children's Hour* when parents begin to remove their children from the school run by the principal characters. As mentioned earlier, the teachers (Audrey Hepburn and Shirley MacLaine) are victims of malicious gossip that has embroiled them in alleged lesbianism. Insisting upon an explanation, Hepburn finally takes one of the fathers aside. Wyler chooses to show this moment of extreme anguish from a distance—over MacLaine's shoulder and through a screen door. The audience can see the father giving an answer but is spared hearing the actual words. Alex North, who wrote the score, omits any music from the sequence. The heavy silence has a far greater effect.

There is a memorable scene in *The Misfits* where Langland (Clark Gable) drunkenly runs out into the street looking for his kids. He climbs on top of a parked car and shouts their names, then collapses. Langland's self-avowed strength and independence suddenly and unexpectedly come apart at the seams for the first time in the story. The intensity of the scene and the expressions of shock on everybody's faces easily carry the shot; music is not needed. (Many actors have pointed to Gable's acting in this scene, describing it as one of the most impressive efforts of his long career.)

In *Citizen Kane* (1941), there is scene in which Kane, at the height of his gubernatorial campaign, has seen a letter his mistress wrote to his wife and is now forced to confront both of them together. This classic confrontation scene is a treacherous moment for Kane; not only is his marriage threatened but so is his political career. Kane, having no idea how he will handle the confrontation, moves through the scene with a deadening sense of dread. There is no music here. The heavy silence imposed through the lack of music causes every word to ring out.

## The Telling Quality of Ambient Sound

Many pictures begin without any musical sound whatsoever. *Catch-22* (1970) is an example of this. The main titles are in black and white, and gradually the silhouette of a jagged, treeless mountain range appears as the sun rises in the background. A dog barks somewhere in the distance. Suddenly, the sound of an airplane engine coughs its way into an idle, interrupting the quietness of the dawn. Soon after, other engines are fired up, first one or two and then, it seems, there are forty or fifty. Ambient sound alone leads the way, evolving into a long sequence showing an entire World War II bomber squadron taking off for an early morning mission.

Ambient sound within a particular environment can mean or say more than words or music could ever hope to say and becomes a kind of music unto itself. The sound of laughing children at play, the purr of a Lamborghini Countach at cruising speed, the slashing of a wounded animal's claws on a frozen pond, and the tumultuous roar of a crowd all have syntax, meaning, and aural poetry of their own. Added musical sound can be a distraction when environmental sounds alone state the case.

*Ambient Sound as Metaphor*

In *The Battle of the Bulge* (1965), composer Benjamin Frankel apparently found no need for music during the first battle sequences. Explosions, machine gun and small arms fire, and the unrelenting racket of the tanks capture the moment. In this case the tanks, like the helicopters in *Apocalypse Now* (1979), exist in part as a metaphor for man's inhumanity to man. Not until the climax of the first attack in *The Battle of the Bulge* is music introduced—the very moment it is needed to amplify the underlying emotion at the sight of human carnage. Finally, the potency of the environmental noise has been reduced by the law of diminishing returns, and the power of music must at last be invoked.

While the use of thunder and lightning to signal an approaching storm is one thing, using these sounds to express the "wrath of God" has been, to say the least, overdone. Yet, their use can still be effective. There is the now-classic scene in the movie *Network* (1976) in which all the citizens in the city lean out of their windows and shout, "I'm mad as hell and I'm not going to take it anymore!" One might expect to hear music reserved for this emotionally charged moment. Instead, thunder and lightning are used—as music. The effect is twofold: The sound is strong because it has its own sense of anger; it is also funny, in an ironic sense, because its use has become so clichéd. Music could well have obscured the tenuous line that this sound effect walks between anger and humor.

*Freeze-Frames*

There is always the chance that an ambient sound has a better chance of working as a metaphor when unencumbered by music. This may be true of certain film editing techniques as well. Freeze-frames, for instance, are sometimes employed at the end of a sequence or at the end of a film to produce an effect of closure. Gene Youngblood has pointed out that "stop-motion is literally the death of an image: we are instantly cut off from the illusion of cinematic life—the immediacy of motion—and the image is suddenly relegated to the motionless past, leaving in its place a pervading aura of melancholy."[2] A good example occurs at the very end of *Fail Safe* (1964). "Stop-motion" shots of adults and of children playing in the streets precede the drop of an atomic bomb on New York City. The final shot of a flock of pigeons sweeping into the air and suddenly halting in freeze-frame substitutes for the actual atomic blast. Significantly, both music and ambient sound were omitted from this ending sequence and end titles. The silence, along with omitted ambient sound for the freeze-frames, produces a heart-stopping effect, originating here with the certainty of death on a massive scale. As Rudolph Arnheim has pointed out, "In the silence of the image, the fragments of a broken vase can talk exactly the way a character talks to his neighbor."[3]

## The Question of Realism

There is a school of thought that believes that a sequence will seem more "real" if it is played without music. While I can think of scenes in which music would have detracted from the realistic flavor of a sequence, I can also recall innumerable moments that have been made *more* real—certainly more dramatic—because music *was* included. It's a matter of context.

Consider the famous shower murder scene from Hitchcock's *Psycho* (1960). The intensity and chilling starkness of the scene, reduced to the bare essentials of a woman's nude body, a porcelain tub, a metal drain and showerhead, a knife blade, and the vague and menacing figure outlined behind an opaque shower curtain, are coupled with a relentless pacing in the editing, cutting between camera angles at a rate averaging less than a second per shot. Because of these two factors, Hitchcock was convinced that the scene should be handled without music. After numerous viewings of the completed film, Hitchcock was forced to admit his error. Though Bernard Herrmann had already completed and recorded the rest of the score, Hitchcock recalled him to create music solely for this scene. The result? One of the most memorable and horrifying moments in screen history, not to mention one of the most often quoted film music cues (in variant forms) ever.

There is a scene from Hitchcock's *Torn Curtain* (1966) involving the murder of Gromek on the farm. Truffaut has described this scene as the most gripping within the film and remarks that "since it is played without music, it is very realistic and also very savage." I have watched the sequence many times, and for the most part I certainly agree with Truffaut. Hitchcock explained that he extended this sequence because he wanted "to show that it [is] very difficult, very painful, and it takes a very long time to kill a man. The public is aware that this must be a silent killing because of the presence of the taxi driver on the farm. Firing a shot is out of the question. . . . We are in a farmhouse and the farmer's wife is doing the killing. So we use household objects: the kettle full of soup, a carving knife, a shovel, and, finally, the gas oven."[4]

Indeed, it is a grisly scene. With just ambient sound, it is easy to be caught up by the grunting and groaning sounds, wheezes and gasps. This puts us into the picture, so to speak, and into the room. However, there is a problem. It is not with how Hitchcock's intention was carried out, but with the intention itself, as experienced within a larger context. In my opinion, realism here—however it may be defined—is out of step with the rest of the film. *Torn Curtain*, like so many of Hitchcock's classic films, is a romantic action/suspense drama. The insertion of stark realism into this film is disruptive, especially in light of Hitchcock's omnipresent signature consisting of touches of humor, elegance, international intrigue, split-second timings and rescues. These latter aspects conspire to move the picture in more theatrical directions.

Herrmann, who had served Hitchcock so well in previous pictures, was originally contracted to write the score but was dropped from the project at the last minute, during the recording session, because of a dispute with Hitchcock. This was a shocking development, considering the monumental successes the two had accrued over their ten-year relationship.

Herrmann's original score was recorded by Elmer Bernstein, and this recording includes the music cue intended for "Gromek's Killing on the Farm." Herrmann must have felt that this scene played more effectively with music, and I wondered why. Taking the liberty of playing the music in rough synchronization with the scene, I was astonished at the results. (I say rough synchronization because, as Bernstein told me, this recording was not destined for the sound track. He therefore picked a tempo that seemed right for the music without worrying about exact metronome indications or timings. Also, I could only guess at the actual intended point of musical entry.) Three things became clear. First, the prolonged time sense Hitchcock sought was shortened by the music. (Music can, after all, change our perception of how time passes.) Second, when Herrmann's music was included, Gromek's pain was made less private. But of greater consequence was that the music brought the scene into line with the point of view of the whole film—that of a romantic action/suspense drama.

John Addison was eventually hired to write the score for *Torn Curtain,* and his score was used for the release print. When Addison and I discussed this scene, I told him my impressions about the point of view and the original score. He said the same thoughts had occurred to him as well. He pointed out, however, that Hitchcock had been adamant about not wanting music for this scene and would brook no argument. Therefore, no music was written for it. As you might infer, agreement on the function of music in a film can be a tricky matter. The same can be said with respect to its absence.

*Chapter Six*

# Practical Matters and the Human Element

In the preceding chapters we have concentrated almost entirely on the question of music's function. To be sure, other matters of a practical nature are involved in film music, and the way these are handled has a decisive influence on the final score. Furthermore, since many highly specialized people are involved in the overall process of film scoring, interactions between them can be a touchy matter. Communication among them is of critical importance. Thus, in this chapter, we will take a summary view of who is involved and the nature of their various responsibilities.

## The Spotting Process

The process begins when the director and the composer "spot" the film to decide where music is needed and why. This usually takes place in the editing room. The music editor attends these meetings to note all decisions as to where music is required—it will be his responsibility to log these places down to the exact frame—and to keep track of other things that are said in the discussions. It is helpful if the film editor is close by because of his intimate knowledge of where tentative cuts have been made and where additional cuts or revisions are under consideration. Ideally, however, the editing has been completed and what exists is the director's cut—the final version.

Preferably, everybody will have seen the film on a large screen. The impact of the images is far greater on a large screen than on a small, television-size editing screen. Not only are the details more discernible, but the pacing

217

also seems different—sometimes slower, sometimes faster, depending upon the context. But the actual spotting usually takes place in front of a flatbed. This machine has fast-forward and reverse capabilities so that the film can be stopped on a precise frame. It registers the location of each frame in terms of footage and seconds. Even though the image appears on a small screen, the flatbed provides a means for making precise choices. This is where the real discussions begin.

*Dramatic Vision and the Director*

Directors' comments are crucial. Their vision of the film, what they are trying to get across, and where they feel the problems are, form a foundation and a direction for the score and can trigger musical thoughts and ideas. Thus, what is said in these meetings has a decisive influence on the overall musical approach.

In these talks, composers test their ideas about the film and suggest what might be attempted with the music. They may have read the script beforehand and developed a certain approach prior to the screening. The spotting session is the time to find out if these ideas are in line with the director's point of view.

It is important to realize that the scoring of a film is a horrendous time for filmmakers because this is when they lose control of the film. In every other stage of the production—acting, lighting, staging, photography, and so on—they have, in effect, the last word. Unless a director is a trained musician who is able to evaluate the score before it is recorded, the final musical decisions are entrusted to the composer. Thus, the spotting sessions are often fraught with anxiety.

Many composers have said that they encourage filmmakers to talk in aesthetic terms rather than in the composer's language. For example, the director might point out that the essence of a certain scene is one of joy in accomplishment, but overdoing this musically would be a mistake, considering what happens in the next scene. This is helpful. However, if a director goes on to say that the music should be written in a style that reminds us of 1932, and that it should be played on a clarinet, the composer will say, "Wait a minute, which style of 1932? There were many. And which clarinet: an E♭ soprano, a B♭, or a bass clarinet? All this makes a difference." Furthermore, when directors are so specific, they run the risk of eliminating choices that would have emerged within an informed and creative musical approach. Richard Rodney Bennett put it this way: "The hardest director to work for is somebody who thinks he knows a little bit about music and who has preconceived ideas about it. Then you're in trouble."[1]

Composers prefer to interpret what the filmmaker is saying and translate this into musical terms. It is best when directors talk about *what* they want the music to do, not how they want it done.

The most effective filmmakers have a clear vision of what they want in a film—and this vision corresponds to what they have in the camera. There are directors who have an almost genius-like sense in this regard. They know what their films are about, and they can express their thoughts in vivid terms. Some are open to new or different approaches, and they are quick to grasp the unique value or appropriateness of musical interaction with a film. John Williams feels that "the best directors are musical; I think part of what they do is musical. The art of editing film in my mind is a musical art."[2] Composers have a kind of marriage with such directors that is not unlike the kind of relationship directors have with actors they use over and over. There is a special communication between them. David Raksin holds Vincente Minnelli in highest esteem, and Alex North speaks warmly about his collaborations with John Huston, as does Leonard Rosenman about Nicholas Ray and Elia Kazan.

*Problems of Communication*

A problem arises with directors whose vision of their films is not as clear as it could or should be, or who ask things of the composer that are outside the context of the picture. As has been said, music is an almost indispensable aid in bringing the intent of a film in line with the final result. But music cannot provide something that is not there, explicitly or implicitly, and still fit the picture. One director said he wanted a spiritual kind of music, but when asked where, he couldn't find a place. If the composer had complied without protest, the score would only have confused the issue. The hope for an alliance between director and composer deteriorates in such situations.

A similar problem exists when there is a confusion about what, in concrete terms, music is capable of expressing. As discussed in Chapter 1, music is a subjective art form. It cannot evoke a picture of something concrete, nor can it express specific literary ideas. For instance, consider a story about a man who is aging. Music cannot express that he would like to be younger. That is a literary idea. Nevertheless, requests of this sort emerge from time to time even on the highest levels of filmmaking. One of the best-known directors of our time said he wanted "lesbian" music for a particular scene. Miffed, the composer confessed that he didn't have the slightest idea what that was.

Sometimes there are disagreements in the spotting sessions as to where the music should be. Pointing to specific scenes, a director might say that we need it here, but we don't need it there. Composers will honor these demands. However, if they feel even marginally convinced that a scene needs music at a certain point, even though it was not asked for, they might write it anyway and give the director a choice in the dubbing. I have done that and was glad of it later on; the director subsequently decided that music was needed after all, and we were spared the expense of having to rehire the musicians to record it.

In spotting the film, it is extremely important to keep an eye on the overall distribution of the music cues as it relates to the dramatic shape or curve of the film. Rosenman feels that generally you can't have too much space between one cue and another. "You have to spread it so that the music becomes a kind of musical spine to the film. Then you have a sense of proportion. You feel that a certain scene belongs here, the development belongs there, and you get a kind of large picture."[3]

Later on, when the composition of the score is underway, directors often want to hear the thematic material in advance of the recording, and they ask to have it played on the piano. Composers generally don't like to do this. In most cases, the themes have been conceived for orchestra. Unless a director can imagine what a given instrumentation sounds like, the music as played on the piano will not represent the composer's intentions, and it won't seem quite right to the director. In reaction to this situation, film-makers have resorted to "temp tracks."

*Temp Tracks*

There are two words that will strike horror in a composer's heart: "temp track." A temp track is prerecorded music that a filmmaker has temporarily placed on the sound track of the work print to take the place of the forth-coming score. There are at least three reasons filmmakers do this, and each is understandable, up to a point.

First, temp tracks can be an aid in the film editing process. When cutting various scenes, editors are inevitably confronted with problems of pacing. They have to decide how long each shot is held, and they know that music will have a bearing on their decisions. (For instance, a shot can be held a bit longer when musical sound is involved.) So they sometimes select what they consider the most appropriate kind of music for a scene and cut with that in mind.

Second, toward the completion of the edit, producers are anxious to show what they have to potential distributors. And they know that the film will make a better impression if there is at least some music on the sound track. That is a practical matter. Third, and this has a direct bearing on the spotting process, directors often feel that their considered choice of temporary music enables them to better communicate to the composer their idea of what they want in the score. They may feel that they lack the formal musical training or background to describe in words what they imagine as music for the film; thus, they choose to play a recording of something so that the composer can take it from there.

While one can readily appreciate these reasons for developing a temp track, it is equally important to consider the problems that result from this approach. For one thing, if the editor has been too circumspect about cutting a sequence to the temp track it might mean that the score would have to move in almost the same way. This raises expectations of the score that are virtually impossible to shake off. But of far greater consequence is the aesthetic burden composers must face in this situation. This happens when filmmakers become so enamored of the temp track—they have heard it over and over again, and they are used to it—that nothing else seems right. I can't think of anything that would more inhibit a composer or more effectively dislodge his or her creative process. Every film composer I know has been in this situation, and they all say that, at a certain point, something inside them rebels or gives up. Certainly, this goes against the best interest of the score and of the film.

*An Ongoing Approach*

Spotting sessions take different forms, depending upon the people involved. Each director has a unique way of working. For each of the two films I did with Robert Altman, he first gave me the script and asked me to jot down my thoughts about the potential use of music. Many composers don't like to do this, because they fear they might conjure up ideas that will conflict with the film version. Richard Rodney Bennett is clear on this issue: "The first time I see a movie I am deliberately, completely blank in my mind. I don't like to read scripts because if I do, I start to come to a movie with cunning ideas about what the music can do."[4] When questioned about this matter, Bernard Herrmann answered: "I could never work from a script when scoring a Hitchcock film; it's Hitch's timing that creates the suspense. You can't guess his musical requirements ahead of time."[5] Others prefer to know about the story in some detail first, so that they can absorb the literary issues before becoming involved with the visual impact of what is on the screen.

It was Altman's practice to screen what had been assembled and trimmed—two or three reels—so as to keep in absolute touch with what the picture looked like on the large screen. These were rough cuts subject to subsequent editing. Everyone involved in the post-production process attended the screenings.

Afterward, I would sketch for several hours in light of what had captured my imagination. Sketching involves writing a few measures of something, the beginning of a phrase or a motivic gesture harmonized and orchestrated in different ways. This may sound like fun and, in a way, it is. But it is also one of the most difficult tasks—if not the most excruciating—in the process, because it is so important to find the melodic shape or sound that will readily attach itself to a particular situation or combination of characters. Sometimes the ideas come in an instant, and often the best ones do. But if they don't, or if what the composer has dreamt up doesn't "make it" at all, then what?

In *Fool for Love*, for example, the first cue is a single line for bass flute. It is a simple enough line that shouldn't have been difficult to write. Yet, I'm embarrassed to say, it took me days to get it to where it seemed right. The tricky thing for me was that I wanted it to have linear and harmonic implications that could be realized elsewhere, and the rhythm had to be expressive of a certain level of nervous energy. As it turned out, the line became the basis for the entire score. This experience was particularly agonizing: I had five weeks to compose thirty to forty minutes of orchestral music and had spent several valuable days composing only a short piece for solo flute and a few scattered sketches showing its potential use.

Often I looked in on the editing room, where at least three editors were up to their elbows in film. Altman, sitting at a flatbed, worked with one for a while, then moved into the next room to work with someone else. He said such things as, "Let's cut here," and then he would mark the frame. Or, "We'd better go to that other shot we have for this," and pointing to shelves loaded with boxes of film he would say, "It's in that box right there."[6]

Altman, like many directors, likes to have many alternative shots of a scene so that in the editing, through the process of attrition, he can distill everything down to the final version. Early on in *Fool for Love*, he formed an overall structural plan that had a decisive influence on the pacing. He said, "This film has to have a kind of staircase shape that begins rather slowly and accumulates. Any letup along the way will wreck the thing."[7] This kind of direction composers find helpful. What kept me at the edge of my seat, however, was knowing the film had not been put together yet, and at this early stage I could only guess what this concept meant for the music down the line.

My time in the editing room, watching the cuts and listening to the discussions, was illuminating. Occasionally Altman would turn to me and say, "I want you to help me out here. I need the whole shot, but here [pointing to a particular frame], I need an ictus or something to pull it together." Or he would say, "Look, it's nighttime—I mean, it is pitch black—and we've got this little girl in the middle of a field. It may not seem particularly threatening to us, but it could be to the girl and I want you to do something with it." He meant that I should play it from her point of view. Looking at the work print, he suggested that I write a sound that would "build to this point, dwindle, and [rolling ahead on the flatbed] come out of it right here."[8] This was what I needed to know. In this manner, I also got the timings for various cues and could proceed with the actual score. This is how the "spotting" went, as the film was being cut.

Eventually the editing raced ahead of me, and one day, when I was beginning to feel the pressure of a deadline—the date for the recording was set and the musicians had been hired—I asked Altman if he could give me a few one-on-one hours so that we could spot some of the finished reels. At that time he was totally absorbed with the ending of the film, and I felt uncomfortable about asking him to go back to an earlier section. But, understanding my dilemma, he spent the time with me.

There probably are numerous composers who wouldn't want to do it this way, preferring to wait until the entire picture is finished before beginning work on the score. I can see many advantages in that approach. But, in this instance, I felt that in a small way I was a part of the process, not somebody who had stepped in at the last moment when everyone else had finished. I also knew more about the intent of the film than if I had seen only the finished print a couple of times.

Bob Altman, like many directors, is involved in every aspect of his films, including the editing. Nobody in the editing room puts in more hours than he, and if someone is dragging around, that person is dismissed. Altman, like any top director, has a vision for each of his films, and he involves each person on a "need to know" basis. When someone disagrees, Altman listens to the opinion and gives thought to the ideas, but certainly he makes the final decision.

I have gone into this much detail about a personal experience not because it is unique, but because I want to point up that the spotting process is not always some kind of cut-and-dried routine that takes place at a few meetings. In reality, it can, and very often does, take many different forms.

## Timings

The music editor plays a major role in timings. He keeps track of the places where music is to be brought in. These places are identified by reel number, footage and frame, and given cue numbers. The music editor logs the whole film in this manner and writes out what is often called a film breakdown sheet. This sheet includes a short description of the dialogue or action and the precise durations of each cue. For instance, the sheet may take on the following appearance:

*Film Breakdown Sheet*

Reel One

| | | |
|---|---|---|
| M.1 *(music cue number)* | *(description)* | 136+12 *(footage/frame)* |
| :46 *(duration in seconds)* | | |
| M.2 | *(description)* | 443+6 |
| :23 | etc. | |

Composers generally like to have the film breakdown as soon as possible so that they can begin to piece together the overall requirements of the score—that is, the different kinds and duration of music needed. This also allows them to work up a schedule of sorts. They tend to dwell on this latter point and for good reason: the deadline. When asked about a picture they are about to do, they often sum it up by saying something like "It's an interesting story that takes place in Australia and I've got about forty-five minutes to write by June 6!"

Creating the cue breakdown or cue sheet, as it is sometimes called, is the next crucial task for the music editor, who must take each cue and describe everything that takes place: action, dialogue, and, where possible, any ambient sounds, such as slamming doors. These events are timed down to a fraction of a second. For instance:

## Cue Sheet

| Timing | Name of cue |
| --- | --- |
| (*in seconds*)   :00 | l.s. (long shot) of ship entering harbor |
| 4:32 | m.s. (medium shot) of deck |
| 8:36 | Cut to bridge |
| 10:79 | c.u. (close-up) of captain, he takes a swig of coffee |
| 11:50 | Captain turns to first mate |
| 12:22 | Capt. says, "Last port is always the best." |
| 13:66 | Two bells sound |
| 15:10 | He says, "Have the Bos'n come to the bridge." |
| 16:54 | Cut to l.s. of harbor as seen from bridge |
| 17:97 | Cut to passageway: crew noisily "turning to" |

It will appear obvious that timings of this sort are exceedingly precise. How could anybody expect to bring music into tight synchronization with numbers like this? The problem is not as serious as it might seem. We know that one-third of a second approaches the point at which we are unable to perceive any mismatch between image and musical sound. Therefore, it is common practice to round off the timings to the nearest third of a second. This makes it easier for the composer and the conductor.

It is helpful to have timings that go beyond the tentatively decided end point, and with good reason. The composer may want the end of a phrase to overlap with the next shot or scene, tying the two together. Suppose, for example, that a music cue is required for a section in which there is no dialogue and that it leads up to the point when somebody says his first line. A musical extension could overlap with the first few words. As mentioned in Chapter 3, the emotional quality of the section without dialogue would then carry over into the opening line. In any case, an extended timing sheet can keep the composer informed when and if such possibilities arise.

### Action, Dialogue, Ambient Sound

It is unlikely that every indication in the cue sheet will be synchronized with a musical event. Composers invariably check only certain things they want to "hit." But it is important that they know when everything in the sequence takes place. Otherwise, embarrassing accidents can occur. For instance, suppose the editor fails to notate that the captain takes a swig of coffee at 10:79 seconds and the composer, forgetting this detail, writes a harp glissando. The "Mickey Mouse" result—where, as in cartoons, the music seems to mimic every action—could be devastating to the whole cue and cause the composer no small amount of anguish when the music is cut into the film.

When there is music with dialogue, there is always the danger that the music will mask the words (even with the volume of the music turned down) by being in rhythmic or textural conflict. So, while it is important to know where the dialogue begins and ends (marked EOL, or end of line, in the cue sheet), it is equally important to know where the pauses or breath points are. As has been pointed out, composers attempt to work with the dialogue in a discreet manner via subtle shifts in the harmony or the initiation of a motivic idea at a pivotal point. Exact timings in this case are essential.

Much the same can be said about the action and ambient sound. Unless the timing sheets indicate precisely where crashes of any sort take place, there is always a chance that such sounds could obliterate an effective musical line. Unfortunately, many ambient sounds are added after the score has been written, and this is a nagging concern. Composers would much rather work around the ambient sounds from the onset than be surprised by them in the dubbing. If, for instance, the final sound track consists of a relentless swell of uproarious pandemonium, one might ask why music was required in the first place. As Alex North once advised me, about the only musical sound that can cut through absolute pandemonium is French horns in unison, preferably in the upper register.

### Camera Motion and Off-Camera Dialogue

The cue sheets should indicate what the camera catches on film. For instance, it is necessary to know if the camera roams around the environment or, certainly, if it flashes back to another time or place during a dialogue. This places the visual content in juxtaposition with the off-camera spoken line—which, in itself, presents an opportunity for the music.

An interesting problem arises when the camera slowly pans across an environment or tilts from low to high. Elements that are judged to be dramatically significant only gradually come into view. The question is: Do you time the appearance of the element from the instant it enters the frame? Or do you wait until it is in full view, so that its meaning can be clearly felt? There is no single answer, but an experienced music editor will take the question into consideration when indicating the timings. He may, for example, say where the image enters and then where, in his estimation, it begins to make an impact. A composer will draw his own conclusion as to how and where he wants to deal with the problem within the indicated boundaries.

## Reel Changes

It is necessary to be aware of reel changes in the spotting. The average length of a reel is about ten minutes. A film lasting 120 minutes is, accordingly, placed on twelve reels, which results in eleven reel changes. Some theaters splice every other reel together, resulting in five changes during the screening. A few theaters place the whole film on one huge reel, which eliminates the necessity for any changes. In any case, the film editor will plan reel changes at specific points, depending on the amount of time available on the reel and where a shot can absorb a slightly shorter or longer duration. His decision is made irrespective of what has been tentatively planned for the music track. The composer's problem is that he must allow for a slight pause in the music at the point of change. Otherwise, a distortion or bleep will occur. If any pause in the music proves too disruptive, a composer may ask the editor if another spot in the film can be found for the change. His request may fall on deaf ears, but it's worth a try.

## Source Music

The timings for source music cues are almost always a simpler matter. As described in Chapter 2, source music originates with the drama (when the car radio is turned on, for example). Therefore, the music editor need only provide the overall duration, along with any major shifts in the action or drama. For source music, composers usually write more music than is required. There are several reasons for this. For one thing, in the real world, music of this sort is rarely heard from its opening measures. When we turn on our car radio or enter an elevator, chances are the music, or Muzak, is already in progress. Thus, in the dubbing, it is frequently more appropriate to bring in source music not at its very beginning but somewhere in the middle. Starting from the beginning could draw unwanted attention to the music. For another thing, the source music could get too busy at the wrong place or even begin to pulsate metrically in too close a correspondence with the dialogue or action. In this case, the dubbing editor would want the latitude to move the cue in one direction or the other until it locks into place. Finally, there always exists the possibility that the scene might be lengthened in the final cut. Having sufficient music to work with then would be crucial.

It is necessary to date all timings in order to avoid confusion when additional cuts are made. Every composer has had calls from the editing room telling him that in a particular cue a certain number of frames have been dropped or reinstated. Composers are likely to be confused after several calls unless all these changes have been clearly noted. Music editors become a valuable, if not essential, asset in this situation.

Some composers choose to write out the timings themselves by watching a videocassette print of the film that has an ongoing tabulation of time, measured in fractions of seconds (known as SMPTE), appearing at the bottom of the screen. Charles Gross, a successful New York–based film composer, prefers this method because he feels more comfortable viewing a scene several times and picking out only those elements that are important to him. He doesn't want to be distracted by the extraneous elements noted by someone else.

Other composers, such as Elmer Bernstein, prefer to work with both a video print and timings from the music editor. With a VCR at their side, they can then review the scene as many times as they need and even play the music along with it. They can always check with the timing sheet for exact timings.

## Synchronization

Once the timings have been determined there remains the question of how they can be used. The process involves bringing hard numbers into relation with musical ideas and the tempi. Generally, an approximate tempo is arrived at in perhaps an unconscious or intuitive manner based on the nature of the chosen musical material and the dramatic impulse. Ernest Gold has said that the tempo comes to him before the notes. "There is a chemistry which takes place when the tempo is right."[9] Others say that the musical ideas at an approximate tempo come to mind first.

### An Exact Tempo

At some early point, it is necessary to determine an exact tempo. The actual writing of the score cannot take place until this decision is made. Given an imagined tempo, composers can only plan what they are going to do at strategic points in the cue, but they can't proceed until the final tempo is established. Once this is done, everything in the music has to lock into place with the film. If it doesn't, the composer has to consider changes of tempi within a cue (which will create serious problems in the recording session) or start over again—and there is little time for that.

Composers have different ways of determining a final tempo. Alex North believes it is useful to consult Bruce Knudson's book, *Project Tempo,*[10] when attempting a tight synchronization, "where the music has to be right on the button." This book shows the relationship between tempo, timing, and beat based on the speed of 35mm film, and it can be used in the following way. Let us consider the short scenario described a few pages back about the captain on the bridge of a ship. Suppose a composer has a rough idea of the kind of music he wants to write and that an approximate tempo in which a quarter note equals between 80 and 86 seems about right. For manageability, composers tend to look for a tempo in which pivotal points requiring special attention fall on a beat. They can always work from there. The Knudson book consists of 241 charts, each representing a tempo ranging from a metronomic pulse of 40 to one of 240 beats per minute. The charts will show that a metronomic beat of 83.48 will accommodate almost every instance in the timing sheet. Various events will fall on the beat, or as close to it as necessary. Furthermore, the charts will show that the cue will consist of 65 beats—valuable information. (See Ex. VI.1.)

*Click Track*

Obviously, 83.48 (rounded off to 84) is a precise numerical value, and no conductor could hope to zero in on and maintain it without help of some kind. But if absolute synchronicity is a vital concern, it is necessary to find ways to achieve this kind of accuracy in the recording. The most reliable method is the use of a click track. Clicks represent beats at a given tempo. They are heard by the conductor and performing musicians through headphones. The mechanically produced clicks enable the musicians to maintain a precise tempo without any variance.

In the past, a click track was prepared by punching holes along the edge of a film. These holes produced a clicking sound that the conductor could hear through his headphone. The clicks represented beats timed at a specific tempo. Clicks are now produced by a digital metronome that can be switched to any tempo, down to a hundredth of a second. This device has replaced the laborious task of punching literally thousands of holes into film.

However, a serious problem emerges with the extended use of click tracks. Invariably, they impose a mechanical quality in the musical performance. Obviously, a symphonic conductor would never consider using this device, since he would want to take liberties with the tempo whenever he felt it appropriate. Still, it is amazing how some experienced studio conductors and players arrive at such effective musical results in spite of the constant click reverberating in their ears.

Ex. VI.1. *Beats to Seconds*

THE TEMPO IS 17.250 FRAMES PER BEAT (17-2), METRONOME—83.48

| click # | 0 | 1 | 2 | 3 | 4 | 5 | 6 | 7 | 8 | 9 |
|---|---|---|---|---|---|---|---|---|---|---|
| 0 | 0.00 | 0.00 | 0.72 | 1.44 | 2.16 | 2.88 | 3.59 | 4.31 | 5.03 | 5.75 |
| 10 | 6.47 | 7.19 | 7.91 | 8.63 | 9.34 | 10.06 | 10.78 | 11.50 | 12.22 | 12.94 |
| 20 | 13.66 | 14.38 | 15.09 | 15.81 | 16.53 | 17.25 | 17.97 | 18.69 | 19.41 | 20.13 |
| 30 | 20.84 | 21.56 | 22.28 | 23.00 | 23.72 | 24.44 | 25.16 | 25.88 | 26.59 | 27.31 |
| 40 | 28.03 | 28.75 | 29.47 | 30.19 | 30.91 | 31.63 | 32.34 | 33.06 | 33.78 | 34.50 |
| 50 | 35.22 | 35.94 | 36.66 | 37.38 | 38.09 | 38.81 | 39.53 | 40.25 | 40.97 | 41.69 |
| 60 | 42.41 | 43.13 | 43.84 | 44.56 | 45.28 | 46.00 | 46.72 | 47.44 | 48.16 | 48.88 |
| 70 | 49.59 | 50.31 | 51.03 | 51.75 | 52.47 | 53.19 | 53.91 | 54.63 | 55.34 | 56.06 |
| 80 | 56.78 | 57.50 | 58.22 | 58.94 | 59.66 | 60.38 | 61.09 | 61.81 | 62.53 | 63.25 |
| 90 | 63.97 | 64.69 | 65.41 | 66.13 | 66.84 | 67.56 | 68.28 | 69.00 | 69.72 | 70.44 |
| 100 | 71.16 | 71.88 | 72.60 | 73.31 | 74.03 | 74.75 | 75.47 | 76.19 | 76.91 | 77.63 |
| 110 | 78.35 | 79.06 | 79.78 | 80.50 | 81.22 | 81.94 | 82.66 | 83.38 | 84.10 | 84.81 |
| 120 | 85.53 | 86.25 | 86.97 | 87.69 | 88.41 | 89.13 | 89.85 | 90.56 | 91.28 | 92.00 |
| 130 | 92.72 | 93.44 | 94.16 | 94.88 | 95.60 | 96.31 | 97.03 | 97.75 | 98.47 | 99.19 |
| 140 | 99.91 | 100.63 | 101.35 | 102.06 | 102.78 | 103.50 | 104.22 | 104.94 | 105.66 | 106.38 |
| 150 | 107.10 | 107.81 | 108.53 | 109.25 | 109.97 | 110.69 | 111.41 | 112.13 | 112.85 | 113.56 |
| 160 | 114.28 | 115.00 | 115.72 | 116.44 | 117.16 | 117.88 | 118.60 | 119.31 | 120.03 | 120.75 |
| 170 | 121.47 | 122.19 | 122.91 | 123.63 | 124.35 | 125.06 | 125.78 | 126.50 | 127.22 | 127.94 |
| 180 | 128.66 | 129.38 | 130.10 | 130.81 | 131.53 | 132.25 | 132.97 | 133.69 | 134.41 | 135.13 |
| 190 | 135.85 | 136.56 | 137.28 | 138.00 | 138.72 | 139.44 | 140.16 | 140.88 | 141.60 | 142.31 |
| 200 | 143.03 | 143.75 | 144.47 | 145.19 | 145.91 | 146.63 | 147.35 | 148.07 | 148.78 | 149.50 |
| 210 | 150.22 | 150.94 | 151.66 | 152.38 | 153.10 | 153.82 | 154.53 | 155.25 | 155.97 | 156.69 |
| 220 | 157.41 | 158.13 | 158.85 | 159.57 | 160.28 | 161.00 | 161.72 | 162.44 | 163.16 | 163.88 |
| 230 | 164.60 | 165.32 | 166.03 | 166.75 | 167.47 | 168.19 | 168.91 | 169.63 | 170.35 | 171.07 |
| 240 | 171.78 | 172.50 | 173.22 | 173.94 | 174.66 | 175.38 | 176.10 | 176.82 | 177.53 | 178.25 |
| 250 | 178.97 | 179.69 | 180.41 | 181.13 | 181.85 | 182.57 | 183.28 | 184.00 | 184.72 | 185.44 |
| 260 | 186.16 | 186.88 | 187.60 | 188.32 | 189.03 | 189.75 | 190.47 | 191.19 | 191.91 | 192.63 |
| 270 | 193.35 | 194.07 | 194.78 | 195.50 | 196.22 | 196.94 | 197.66 | 198.38 | 199.10 | 199.82 |
| 280 | 200.53 | 201.25 | 201.97 | 202.69 | 203.41 | 204.13 | 204.85 | 205.57 | 206.28 | 207.00 |
| 290 | 207.72 | 208.44 | 209.16 | 209.88 | 210.60 | 211.32 | 212.03 | 212.75 | 213.47 | 214.19 |
| 300 | 214.91 | 215.63 | 216.35 | 217.07 | 217.79 | 218.50 | 219.22 | 219.94 | 220.66 | 221.38 |
| 310 | 222.10 | 222.82 | 223.54 | 224.25 | 224.97 | 225.69 | 226.41 | 227.13 | 227.85 | 228.57 |
| 320 | 229.29 | 230.00 | 230.72 | 231.44 | 232.16 | 232.88 | 233.60 | 234.32 | 235.04 | 235.75 |
| 330 | 236.47 | 237.19 | 237.91 | 238.63 | 239.35 | 240.07 | 240.79 | 241.50 | 242.22 | 242.94 |
| 340 | 243.66 | 244.38 | 245.10 | 245.82 | 246.54 | 247.25 | 247.97 | 248.69 | 249.41 | 250.13 |
| 350 | 250.85 | 251.57 | 252.29 | 253.00 | 253.72 | 254.44 | 255.16 | 255.88 | 256.60 | 257.32 |
| 360 | 258.04 | 258.75 | 259.47 | 260.19 | 260.91 | 261.63 | 262.35 | 263.07 | 263.79 | 264.50 |
| 370 | 265.22 | 265.94 | 266.66 | 267.38 | 268.10 | 268.82 | 269.54 | 270.25 | 270.97 | 271.69 |
| 380 | 272.41 | 273.13 | 273.85 | 274.57 | 275.29 | 276.00 | 276.72 | 277.44 | 278.16 | 278.88 |
| 390 | 279.60 | 280.32 | 281.04 | 281.75 | 282.47 | 283.19 | 283.91 | 284.63 | 285.35 | 286.07 |
| 400 | 286.79 | 287.51 | 288.22 | 288.94 | 289.66 | 290.38 | 291.10 | 291.82 | 292.54 | 293.26 |
| 410 | 293.97 | 294.69 | 295.41 | 296.13 | 296.85 | 297.57 | 298.29 | 299.01 | 299.72 | 300.44 |

| click # | 0 | 1 | 2 | 3 | 4 | 5 | 6 | 7 | 8 | 9 |
|---|---|---|---|---|---|---|---|---|---|---|
| 420 | 301.16 | 301.88 | 302.60 | 303.32 | 304.04 | 304.76 | 305.47 | 306.19 | 306.91 | 307.63 |
| 430 | 308.35 | 309.07 | 309.79 | 310.51 | 311.22 | 311.94 | 312.66 | 313.38 | 314.10 | 314.82 |
| 440 | 315.54 | 316.26 | 316.97 | 317.69 | 318.41 | 319.13 | 319.85 | 320.57 | 321.29 | 322.01 |
| 450 | 322.72 | 323.44 | 324.16 | 324.88 | 325.60 | 326.32 | 327.04 | 327.76 | 328.47 | 329.19 |
| 460 | 329.91 | 330.63 | 331.35 | 332.07 | 332.79 | 333.51 | 334.22 | 334.94 | 335.66 | 336.38 |
| 470 | 337.10 | 337.82 | 338.54 | 339.26 | 339.97 | 340.69 | 341.41 | 342.13 | 342.85 | 343.57 |
| 480 | 344.29 | 345.01 | 345.72 | 346.44 | 347.16 | 347.88 | 348.60 | 349.32 | 350.04 | 350.76 |
| 490 | 351.47 | 352.19 | 352.91 | 353.63 | 354.35 | 355.07 | 355.79 | 356.51 | 357.22 | 357.94 |
| 500 | 358.66 | 359.38 | 360.10 | 360.82 | 361.54 | 362.26 | 362.98 | 363.69 | 364.41 | 365.13 |
| 510 | 365.85 | 366.57 | 367.29 | 368.01 | 368.73 | 369.44 | 370.16 | 370.88 | 371.60 | 372.32 |
| 520 | 373.04 | 373.76 | 374.48 | 375.19 | 375.91 | 376.63 | 377.35 | 378.07 | 378.79 | 379.51 |
| 530 | 380.23 | 380.94 | 381.66 | 382.38 | 383.10 | 383.82 | 384.54 | 385.26 | 385.98 | 386.69 |
| 540 | 387.41 | 388.13 | 388.85 | 389.57 | 390.29 | 391.01 | 391.73 | 392.44 | 393.16 | 393.88 |
| 550 | 394.60 | 395.32 | 396.04 | 396.76 | 397.48 | 398.19 | 398.91 | 399.63 | 400.35 | 401.07 |
| 560 | 401.79 | 402.51 | 403.23 | 403.94 | 404.66 | 405.38 | 406.10 | 406.82 | 407.54 | 408.26 |
| 570 | 408.98 | 409.69 | 410.41 | 411.13 | 411.85 | 412.57 | 413.29 | 414.01 | 414.73 | 415.44 |
| 580 | 416.16 | 416.88 | 417.60 | 418.32 | 419.04 | 419.76 | 420.48 | 421.19 | 421.91 | 422.63 |
| 590 | 423.35 | 424.07 | 424.79 | 425.51 | 426.23 | 426.94 | 427.66 | 428.38 | 429.10 | 429.82 |

*Free Timing*

There are alternatives to the click track, and two of these fall under the heading of free timing: recording to a stopwatch, and picture cueing. Conducting with a stopwatch is the simplest approach. It usually requires a clock placed in front of the conductor's stand, which is large enough (about a foot in diameter) so that it can be seen from the corner of his eye. His attention is on the score itself, which contains the timings. Sometimes he will have the film projected on a large screen placed behind the orchestra, so that he can be guided by the picture as well.

Picture cueing is another method of synchronization. Holes are punched in the film, and these openings allow flashes of light to be seen when the film is run through the projector. The "punches" are placed in places where the music is intended to be in close synchronization. Then diagonal lines called "streamers" are scraped onto the film or drawn in with a grease pencil to cue the conductor. The three-foot-long streamers have a two-second duration. The conductor watches the film during the recording and sees the diagonal line panning across the screen from left to right. When the line reaches the bottom right side, it is followed by the flash of light.

Picture cueing offers many advantages. It allows for a certain amount of musical flexibility in performance and enables the conductor to tie in with the ebb and flow of the picture. In addition, this method, which involves an immediate matching of the two media, lets the composer experience in real time what he has written and see how well it works. If something is not quite right, he can make a few changes in the music, either on the spot or before the next recording session.

Experienced composers prefer picture cueing for all the reasons mentioned above and will look disparagingly upon the young composer who tends to have "click tracks on the brain." Picture cueing is virtually an art unto itself—a performing art—and it requires a fair amount of experience to carry it off. Some composers struggling with their first feature-length films are quick to admit they fear imminent disaster with this method. Any insurance, such as the click track, is welcomed.

### Variables Affecting Perception Time

A subtle aspect of synchronization emerges with the lag in perception time between the instant an image is projected on the screen and the time the viewer sees it. A research optometrist told me it takes about two-fifths of a second for this process to take place. For another thing, it takes a certain amount of time to have some kind of comprehension of what is in the picture. Many variables must be taken into account. The amount of detail in a shot is one factor. Compare a picture of a single bird flying in a cloudless sky with a picture of a stormy sky teeming with flocks of birds flapping their wings in rapid, irregular motion. The former will take less time to comprehend than the latter. The more detail a picture has, the longer it takes for the eye and brain to absorb it.

A vast array of colors in a picture naturally points up many eye-catching elements. Visual comprehension time, in such instances, moves at a slower rate and makes it difficult for the viewer to concentrate on essentials. For this reason (among others), many filmmakers elect to shoot in black and white. It is possible that Peter Ustinov favored black and white for *Billy Budd* (1962) because Melville's story line was so strong as to demand the viewer's complete attention. Details pointed up by color would have only been a distraction. In recent times, colorization has become a contentious issue, and I can't help thinking that objections to it along these lines have some validity, particularly in regard to classic films such as *The Maltese Falcon* (1941), which was conceived in black and white.

Camera placement is an additional factor. A close-up ordinarily requires more time to be fully perceived than does a long shot. Imagine a close-up of a tired, emotionally drained face; it would fill the screen with more detail than would a long shot of the same man standing a hundred yards in the distance. The nature of a series of shots is another issue. If these are arranged so that there is no apparent or immediate connection, each shot will require a greater absorption time than if each shot is an observable link in a continuous chain of thought.

From incipience (the instant the picture is flashed on the screen) to the moment its content is recognized and comprehended, there is a time space consisting of many variables. Musical synchronization with the onset of a projected image takes this into consideration. For an effective result in some instances, editors have found it unwise to line up the onset of recorded sound with the first frame of an image, and composers have planned ahead for a "soft sync." Bringing in the music six or more frames later will often feel much more comfortable.

## Generalized Compositional Approaches

Most of the time, composers are given only four to six weeks to write a score, a nearly impossible time frame considering the amount of music involved. Some have called the act of film composition pure suicide because it involves non-stop, round-the-clock schedules. To make matters worse, composers may spend the first week or so looking for, or experimenting with, different musical ideas, and then they have only three to five weeks to compose and orchestrate the score.

Naturally, composers become totally immersed in the subject of the film. Ernest Gold reveals that after he completed the score to *On the Beach* he went into a real depression. He was exhausted, of course. But more than that, he had written the music behind the deaths of seven people he had grown fond of. A couple of weeks later, he woke up one morning and said to himself, "Wait a minute! What am I doing? That was just a movie!"[11]

Composers approach film scoring in many different ways, depending on their personality and training. Alex North says this about his approach: "I work out a plan in terms of the dramatic line, so that I know where I'm going. I'd work backwards and forwards knowing that I've got to reach certain moments of tension at a certain time. The musical contour has to make sense. I usually pick out the areas which are key to the conflict, which are the soul of the thing, and write them first. I may overwrite them in relation to what precedes and follows, but I can always work that out later." In reference to a detailed approach to each cue, North says, "I respect the essence of the whole scene rather than the momentary flip-flops of the individual. I prefer to write a sustained piece rather than do it vertically." But North emphasizes what is perhaps most important: "I find it practically

impossible to score anything that does not move me emotionally. I attempt
to convey the internal rather than the external aspects of the film."[12]

Leonard Rosenman follows a slightly different approach. "The first thing
I do is separate the cues in terms of length, from the longest to the shortest.
I always take the longest sequence first. Generally it would have the most
complicated and developed music in it. I'm much more interested in development. I get an idea of the largest kind of microcosm of the action of the
film in some way and then determine the music for it. By writing an extended sequence, I'm able to test the material as to what its ramifications
are. In other words, I get a handle on the thing—a gesture, a chord, a
series of ideas, or whatever—and the rest of the score becomes simpler."[13]

Rosenman has said: "When you establish thematic fragments for different situations or people and then bring them together later on in a climactic
scene of some sort, then you know exactly the kind of conflicts that are
going on in the film, because they all have been established. This is the
kind of thing that makes a score more memorable. You don't always have
to have a long line or a kind of theme."[14]

What about the structural growth of the score? Rosenman is adamant on
this issue: "The structural growth is not the growth of the music. It's the
growth of the film."[15]

Ernest Gold has used a unique approach for several of his films. After
viewing a picture, he has tried writing a short, five-minute piece. The
piece consists of various ideas he found suitable for different characters and
situations. By connecting these ideas within a single composition, he has
been able to arrive at a sense of continuity that might not have existed had
he developed each idea separately. With that piece at his side, he has felt
ready to write the score.

David Raksin prefers to write the score in the same order as the film, if
possible. "I'd be writing the music as fast as it comes. Sometimes you can
think of everything ahead of time and sometimes you can't. I'd have a
theme in mind that is associated with something in the picture and another
theme associated with something else, when all of a sudden, two-thirds of
the way through the picture, I find that the two ideas combine almost
effortlessly. I must have thought of that before, but not consciously."[16]

Bernard Herrmann points out that, in addition to the pictures and everything else, the audience receives the actual "physical and mental impetus"
of a musical structure. The musical or formal shape of a cue is a fundamental issue. I asked Ernest Gold about this; he said, "Sometimes a scene corresponds to some kind of musical form, where the natural logic inherent in

music emerges in a well-formed or -shaped scene. Good directors seem to produce such scenes; bad directors produce scenes that go against any musical or dramatic logic or formal shape."[17] Gold is not referring to any specific form—sonata, rondo, and the like—but, rather, to shapes that have beginnings and endings, highs and lows—that is, musical strategies. Well-trained and experienced composers invariably think in terms of large-scale structures. Elements of continuity, contrast, motion, and balance are taken as basic components. It naturally follows that each cue they write would make some kind of musical sense. The extent to which this registers on an audience is arguable. However, I am convinced that the formal logic of a music cue in relation to the film makes an impression that has a positive effect.

Music under dialogue is a tricky matter. There is always the danger that the music will mask the words, and if the words can't be heard, the dubbers will lower the volume, and this means they may lower all of it. Certain things disappear before other things, principally the bass, and you will hear just the oboe or a middle voice. One way around this is to orchestrate under-dialogue music in such a way that the bass is heavier than it ordinarily would be. This is risky, of course. Generally, a good composer will write the music in such a way that the volume doesn't have to be taken down.

John Williams offers the following comment. Music under dialogue "has become a somewhat dated practice. Back in the old Warner days a picture was scored from beginning to end. However, I do find myself scoring dialogue scenes every now and then, and they can be very effective. I think that a composer should think of the dialogue as part of the score, [and the music] as an accompaniment. There are a few tips. For example, if the dialogue has a low string sonority underneath, [this] gives the dialogue something to sit on. This isn't to say that one can't have high frequencies as well. In the end, context, style of the picture, etc., has everything to do with it."[18] Alex North offers an additional comment, particularly in regard to the orchestration for under-dialogue cues: "In most cases, I try to avoid anything that's thick texturewise and all doublings [in the orchestra]. I try for a more-or-less transparent score, depending on the scene."[19]

## Orchestration and the Orchestra

Virtually all professional composers consider composition and orchestration an inseparable act. Bernard Herrmann is clear on this issue: "To orchestrate is like a thumb print. I can't understand having someone else do it. It would be like someone putting color to your paintings."[20] Herrmann's music has a special sound, a special quality that is unique. This is true of Raksin, North, Rosenman, and many other great film composers as well. To be sure, it is difficult if not impossible to tell where their compositional styles leave off and their orchestrational styles begin. This is, of course, a hallmark of a good composer. However, when one considers the excruciating deadlines a film composer must face, it is easy to understand why, in most cases, an orchestrator is needed, particularly for laying out the score. The nature of his role depends upon the composer he has been hired to assist.

*Short Score*

In a traditional sense, the orchestrator is there to save time, a commodity that slips away at frightening speed toward the end of a project. Generally, he works from a short score or "sketch." I asked John Addison to comment on how this works out.

> The orchestrator can mean a lot of different things. On the one hand, if you want to write music for film and all you can do is whistle and hum, then indeed, that is what you do into a tape recorder and the orchestrator will do the rest. You will not, by the way, be admired by the established composers if this is the way you work. To compare this with what a trained composer does is absurd.
>
> In my own case, I write my sketches on eight or nine staves and, to save time, use the orchestrator to transfer this to a full score [where each instrument is assigned a separate stave on the page]. Obviously, it takes less time to write a short score. In *Sleuth*, they didn't, for some extraordinary reason, allow any money for an orchestrator, so I decided to do the score myself, hoping there would be enough time. Halfway through writing it, the money was available. I called up my orchestrator and he got to work. The odd thing is that if I listen to the recording, I can't tell you which ones I scored and which he did.
>
> Everything is in the sketch. It's just that instead of having one line for the flutes, one line for the oboes, one for the clarinets, you can write it all on one line. Occasionally, you can say, "add harp." Sometimes I will say, "add a little percussion, but don't overdo it."
>
> When orchestrating for the woodwinds, for instance, two flutes and two oboes can be voiced either as two on top of the other two, or they can be dovetailed. If you are a composer, you hate to leave that to someone else. It makes a little difference in the sound. If you are in a terrible rush, you will simply write out the chord and say to the

orchestrator to do it in a certain way. Another thing you can do is write out the first few bars exactly the way you want them to be and indicate that this is to be carried out, and then just write out the chords. The same applies to strings and brass.

To some extent, repetition is very typical and useful in film music. Therefore, you can quite legitimately use material over again. But you can put a different beginning on it or a different end. You may even want to change the length of it by putting something in the middle. You can say to the orchestrator, "do that again, but add bassoons to the cellos and basses, because there is going to be more ambient sound and we'll never hear it the other way." These are familiar timesavers.

There are other things they can do. In Hollywood, there are orchestrators who have worked with many different composers. So they probably know one or two tricks that you don't know yourself.[21]

Most composers work in a similar manner. And their compositional "sketches" vary in the amount of detail. Alex North, for instance, likes to leave something up to the orchestrator. "It helps keep his interest up."[22] David Raksin, on the other hand, prefers to put everything into the sketch. Rosenman wrote out the complete score for *Fantastic Voyage* because, for one thing, he had a lot of time, and for another, there was no way of indicating the complex orchestral texture to an orchestrator. In any case, established composers rarely leave aesthetic decisions of any consequence to someone else. Their sketches are, for the most part, complete compositions for orchestra.

Source music cues are a different matter. If the problem is to emulate a given style, personal orchestrational leanings are more or less ruled out. Take, for instance, a source music cue that calls for the sound of a 1940s swing band (Dorsey, Goodman, Basie). The orchestrator might be given only the tune and the instrumentation, and it would be his job to orchestrate it in that stylistic genre. He should be able to do this convincingly. Again, this saves the composer time and allows him to concentrate on more important matters.

The orchestrator is perhaps the only other musician on the project with whom composers can discuss the musical sketches and the various things the music is attempting to do. Many composers try out their ideas on orchestrators and, to a certain extent, depend upon them for firsthand criticism. In this way, an orchestrator becomes a sort of shadow figure or collaborator and, frankly, a valued friend who doesn't fold in times of severe stress. Through repeated assignments, collaborators can grow so close that each knows what the other is thinking. I'm sure this is the case, for instance, with Alex North and Henry Brant or with John Williams and Herbert Spencer.

## Diversity of Styles

Movies are so diversified in subject matter that even a schooled composer can find himself relatively unprepared to "get at" a particular orchestral sound or style demanded for a particular scene. Rosenman confesses that when he first went to Hollywood to write the score for *East of Eden,* he was confronted with the task of writing the main titles music in a style he simply had not studied as a student. He quickly got together with his orchestrator to learn how to do it. Likewise, John Addison did a score for a film in which he was called upon to write a few cues in a Glenn Miller style. He didn't have an orchestrator for that picture, and his background and education had not prepared him to do that. Laughing, he tells how he bought a book showing how it was done and gave himself a crash course.

This understandable problem is familiar to anyone who has composed for movies. If you have grown up in Duluth and are suddenly asked to sketch out two minutes of music for a mariachi band or a Japanese koto ensemble, you may have to do a bit of scrambling. No one is prepared for every contingency. However, the great orchestrators in Hollywood— Herbert Spencer, Arthur Morton, and Edward B. Powell, and those who are known as both orchestrators and composers, such as Friedhofer and Brant—are legendary not only for having developed an incredible understanding of the orchestral medium and the individual instruments, but also for having an amazing resourcefulness and ability to deal with an array of orchestral styles. I have heard their names spoken in the same breath as Berlioz and Strauss!

## Instrumental Combinations

The symphony orchestra is, and virtually has to be, standardized in size: winds and brass by threes and fours, harp, piano, percussion, and strings. Film scores need not conform to this particular instrumental distribution. Composers are free to call for any instrumentation they want or need. Bernard Herrmann's score for *Torn Curtain* calls for twelve flutes, sixteen horns, two tubas, two sets of timpani, eight cellos, and eight basses. There would be no way for a symphony orchestra to assemble that combination for one piece in a single concert without going to great expense.

Ordinarily, studio orchestras consist of between thirty-eight and sixty-five musicians. Sometimes composers require much less and for legitimate reasons. For instance, Ernest Gold said about his score for *Ship of Fools* (1965) that "the decision to write music for a ship's trio was made *for* me in a way, but it seemed to work. It appeared as source."[23] On the question of orchestra size, Bernard Herrmann makes an interesting point that is well worth bearing in mind: "The picture soundtrack is an exquisitely sensitive medium. With skillful engineering, a simple bass flute solo, the pulsing of a bass drum, or the sound of muted horns can be far more effective than half a hundred musicians playing away."[24] On the other hand, composers have written for combinations of immense proportions when the situation demanded it. For example, Alex North used 102 players for *Dragon Slayer* (1981), which is about the same size orchestra Stravinsky used for *The Rite of Spring*. Actually, it is only on rare occasions that a budget will allow for this many players.

Unlike concert music, film music is written only to be recorded, generally over a span of three to four days. Assume that the recording takes place over a three-day period—that is, six three-hour sessions—and that the budget allows for sixty musicians. Musicians are hired by the session, not by the day or for the whole recording. It is irrelevant to the producer who is employed for each session so long as there are no more than sixty musicians in the room at a time. This is why composers can call for any instrumental combination they want for each session. In effect, the overall score could involve six different combinations and give the impression that the orchestra consists of more players than is actually the case at any one time. This possibility is indigenous to the film medium and goes unnoticed by an audience since they only hear the orchestra—they don't see it. It is, however, rarely taken to this extreme. Composers prefer to work within a given combination, because this will bring a sense of continuity to the score. But they can and do make adjustments when necessary.

The exact nature of the instrumental ensembles is planned far in advance of the recording sessions. In practical terms this can involve an approach sometimes called "falloff." For instance, assume that most of the cues call for the full ensemble, whatever that may be. Those cues can be recorded first. Next, there may be cues calling only for strings, winds, and percussion. The brass would be excused for that session. Finally, only strings and one or two winds may be required, and so on until, perhaps, only one player remains on the soundstage to record solo passages. The gradual elimination of players, reminiscent of Haydn's *Farewell* Symphony, is a great money-saver. There is no point in employing musicians for sessions when they are not needed. Furthermore, musicians play better when they are kept busy. There is something debilitating about just standing around. The musicians won't complain, because, after all, they are being paid. But some will grumble, and the atmosphere in the recording studio can become slightly unmanageable.

## Doubling

A first-chair clarinetist in a symphony orchestra will play only B♭ and A clarinets—never the E♭ or bass clarinet. The third-chair clarinetist will do that, but this is about as far as the clarinet section will go. They are specialists, and they naturally feel their ability on one instrument would be compromised by changing back and forth. On the other hand, studio musicians, especially woodwind and percussion players, specialize in doubling on two or more instruments, and they are paid more, in accordance with what they do. Some take a delight in doubling on instruments that are generally not used by symphony orchestras. Thus, film composers can call for these instruments to enlarge their orchestral palette.

For instance, a studio doubler in the woodwind section can be asked to bring a B♭ contrabass clarinet, or even a basset horn, in addition to the other clarinets. The same musician most likely has the different saxophones as well. Over the years, Raksin says he has probably written for just about anything in existence. In the score for *Cleopatra* (1963), Alex North wrote a part for a double bass saxophone, a monstrous instrument over six feet long. Looking at it towering in the middle of the wind section, someone once observed that "if it ever fell off its supporting stand, it would waste about eight guys." The lower register is unique, and you can almost feel the notes approaching before actually hearing them.

Other instruments include the bass flute (which is sometimes but not always used in today's symphony orchestra), the African wooden piccolo, the native American and Inca flutes, the baritone oboe or heckelphone, the recorder (which was used primarily in the Baroque period), and a wide range of string instruments including the banjo, mandolin, hurdy-gurdy, dulcimer, and, of course, the guitar.

Doubling is useful but sometimes troublesome. Some musicians can play several instruments so well it is virtually impossible to tell which one is their primary instrument. In New York, I saw a person who showed up at a recording studio with nine instruments, all of which he played remarkably well. To boot, when the recording session was over and most of the musicians had left the studio, he rounded up the pianist and the two of them read through a few pages of Schubert lieder. He even had an excellent baritone voice. On the other hand, there are many who claim to have doubling capabilities but who, in fact, sound almost like amateurs on their other instruments. This can be disastrous for the composer who planned on a doubling, only to find out too late that it will sound bad. To guard against this, a contractor must have an accurate idea of who plays what and how well before hiring the musicians.

Percussionists in today's symphony orchestra are more flexible, even inventive, than anyone else in the orchestra. A mere listing of the instruments they have would require several pages. But even then they can't be expected to have everything. In films taking place in the Near East, composers have availed themselves of the enormous collection of instruments housed at the Department of Ethnomusicology at UCLA. As Mark Evans mentions, Bronislau Kaper even went to Thailand to collect additional instruments and players when he was engaged to score *Lord Jim*.

The point? Because of the recording aspect, the demands for unique kinds of music, and the flexibility of the "studio musician," film composers have been able to explore different avenues of orchestral sound. The results, in many cases, have been stunning.

## The Synthesizer

The subject of orchestration brings us to the issue of synthesized sound as an addition to the orchestra. By the late 1980s, many films (and virtually everything on television) incorporated the synthesizer. This is not a new development—synthesizers have been used in films since the 1970s—but recent technological advancements have ensured far greater resourcefulness and dependability than before, thus enhancing their usefulness.

One sad note, however, is the fate of the many musicians who had built their lives around being the ideal "studio" musician. The near-monumental surge of the digital synthesizer in the 1980s tragically forced innumerable musicians into unemployment. Some highly accomplished players had to leave Los Angeles altogether in the hope of finding work elsewhere. It was sad to see an entire generation of specialized performers—and, along with them, a specialized performance practice—fade into relative obscurity. In the 1990s, however, there are indications of a turnaround.

### Analogue Synthesizers

Portable analogue synthesizers such as the Arp 2600 became available in the late 1960s. They had severe drawbacks. For example, it was extremely difficult to keep them in tune. The frequency modulating controls would start to drift after eight or ten seconds. Second, while standardized wave shapes were hard-wired (that is, they required only a gating procedure to be heard), sounds that were in any way unique had to be patched in manually via patch cords and slider or attenuator adjustments. This required setup time and on-the-spot experimentation. Worse, there was only faint hope that a particular sound complex could be reproduced a few minutes later, much less the next day. It was considered risky to use these synthesizers for recording sessions, especially when tuned acoustic instruments were involved.

Still, composers were tempted to incorporate the analogue synthesizer in various scores to get timbral effects that were not available in the orchestra. For instance, Alex North used the synthesizer in his score for *Shanks* (1973) to combine a slightly enriched sine tone signal with a woman's voice. The signal was frequency modulated, which produced a fast vibrato, and the doubling with the woman's voice, sung straight, produced just what he needed for the film. In the story, Marcel Marceau plays the part of Shanks, a deaf mute who works for an aging scientist. The scientist shows him how to make dead animals move by remote control. Shanks welcomes the restoration of movement to the dead and he wishes the same could be done for his hearing. The musical sound was a metaphor, combining, in a sense, the living with the mechanical.

Jerry Goldsmith employed the synthesizer in his score for *Tora! Tora! Tora!* In one scene, Admiral Yamamoto verbalizes his regret about proceeding with war plans but finds that the momentum toward carrying them out is too strong for him to intercede. Goldsmith's use of the synthesizer effectively underlines the gravity of the situation. A voltage-controlled filter sweeps a complex low-pitched sound, producing a kind of growl that is unmistakably appropriate for the scene.

In *The Anderson Tapes* (1971), Quincy Jones uses synthesized sound almost exclusively. The electronically generated gestures easily relate to an ongoing aspect of the story, which centers on the illegal taping of conversations concerning a burglary. On occasion, Jones combines the electronic material with a small jazz ensemble. Significantly, the combination of non-pitched sounds with tonal music can work. The ear accepts any tentative pitch discrepancy when the two sound media are brought together into one musical texture.

In *The Conversation* (1974), David Shire used a synthesizer to filter the sound of a piano. The slightly weird effect worked well with scenes showing that Harry's mind was beginning to go. For the dope scene of *Farewell,*

*My Lovely* (1976), Shire generated a sound resembling a tuba and wrote a fast-moving passage in the extreme low register that would have been impossible to play on a conventional instrument.

In the early 1970s, a few of us experimented with electronic sound as played "live" along with a film. The idea was prompted, in part, by the possibility that a synthesizer was capable of producing an almost endless range of timbral sounds; therefore, it was conceivable that one or two synthesizers could, along with a few other instruments, take the place of a "pit" orchestra and, as such, accommodate the various needs of a film. We purchased several short silent films (one-reelers) and proceeded to score them, with the idea of giving concerts. It was an exciting adventure, and we thought we were on the edge of something new. We might have been.

We rehearsed the music for several months. Even though the scores were not that difficult to perform, they became very difficult once the film was rolling. While it was one thing to keep in sync with the drama, it was quite another to achieve the feeling that we were, in a sense, "breathing" with what was occurring on the screen. We couldn't have punches and streamers to guide us, since they would have been distracting to the audience. And we didn't want to resort to a click track, since that would have been distracting to us in our effort to give a "live" performance. The matter of "live" was also complicated because there is no dialogue or ambient sound in silent film. Not only does this eliminate another source of cueing (such as specific words); it also imposes the necessity for continuous music. As mentioned in the previous chapter, once music is introduced in a silent film, any letup or silence results in a near-deathly pall. Therefore, given the problems of the analogue synthesizer, we had to become inventive and practiced in its use. We felt we had achieved a certain amount of success; our audiences, however, had mixed responses.

### Digital Systems

The use of synthesizers in film music underwent massive change with the advent of digital systems in the early 1980s and sampling technology in the late 1980s. Countless problems regarding tuning and routing were solved, and this opened up a range of possibilities that, for all practical purposes, would have been inconceivable with the earlier analogue systems. [*The multiple-voice keyboard, for example, was a decisive improvement. Only one note at a time could be played on the older synthesizer. We also have access to sixteen or more different voices from the keyboard or from any external MIDI controller in terms of tuning, transposition, volume, and timbral assignment. There are internal memory slots for user-created voices and timbres, ruling out the need for patch cords. A precision SMPTE time code generator allows the user to "stripe" an audio or video tape at the beginning of a recording.*

*[Now, an "event" mode allows the user to transmit a specific MIDI program and/or control change messages in synchronization with particular SMPTE addresses received from the master tape. In addition, there are extensive editing capabilities that allow for accelerandi or ritardandi and alternations of a sequence of control changes. In the chase mode, punch-ins are made easier and faster.]*

### "Sweetening"

It is, perhaps, the sampling process that has attracted the most widespread attention. This process involves a digital picture of a given sound, including acoustic sound, and exists as a source of subsequent manipulation. Sampled string sounds have been used to augment or "sweeten" an (acoustic) string section. Often, but with far less convincing results, the sampled string sounds are substituted for a string quintet, involving solo strings.

A near-revolutionary technological advancement has occurred in the area of synthesized sound generation and manipulation, and refinements are taking place daily. It remains to be seen how these advancements will be absorbed and utilized in the future. At present, however, many people object to electronic music when it is intended to sound like an orchestra. Unfortunately, it doesn't sound like orchestral music.

The beauty of electronic music is that it has a different vocabulary from that of orchestral music, and it can do things that an orchestra can't. When it is used *with* an orchestra, unique sounds can be produced, and that is wonderful. Sadly, most producers want electronic music to sound like an orchestra merely to save money. In some films, this may work. But there is something about electronically produced sound (as opposed to acoustic sound) that distances us from an image. For many reasons, a live orchestra registers more intimately with the audience. If this distancing is appropriate, there is no problem. Otherwise, there is no substitute for the sound of an orchestra as we know it.

## Music Mix and Dubbing

After the music has been recorded and the best "takes" have been selected, it is necessary to arrive at the final music mix, which is placed, ordinarily, on one or two tracks. The music mix provides certain opportunities for adjustments in the overall balance. For instance, if the brass is a bit loud, that track can be turned down. A solo instrument, such as a flute in its lower register, may need boosting, especially if the flute part is embedded within a relatively thick orchestral texture. The recording medium allows for adjustments of this kind. However, if this technique is overdone, as it has been in many cases, the results begin to sound unnatural.

The music mix presents additional possibilities that would be unattainable on the concert stage. For example, suppose a score calls for a unique combination of exotic instruments that require an inordinate amount of time and experimentation to set up. There is no need to deal with this during a normal recording session, and it would be far too costly to try. Their track can be recorded at a separate time and added to the final mix. This is possible for synthesized tracks as well.

It is at the dubbing stage that the final miracles take place. This is the time when each cue is placed alongside its designated place on the film. Included, eventually, are the dialogue and ambient sound tracks. It is, to say the very least, a dramatic moment in the whole process. After weeks and sometimes months of planning and worrying, here it is. You can see it and you can hear it. Up to this point, these scenes have only been viewed "dry" (without music)—unless, of course, there had been a temp track. But now these scenes suddenly come to life, they move in slightly different ways, and there is more of a sense of drama. In other words, the music is actually doing what it is supposed to be doing. Also, the music itself seems different. It's no longer music that is supposed to go with something else; it has another value and sound. It now belongs with something else. Of course, the dubbing takes place on a flatbed, which has a small screen and very small speakers. It is a different matter when the film is screened in a theater with an audience.

Problems arise in the dubbing stage when determining the viability of each cue. These have to be solved. Fortunately, the composer is not working without a net, so to speak. If the music seems to fit like a glove, that is one thing. If, on the other hand, there seems to be discrepancy or conflict, there are several things to try. One is to realign the placement of the cue by moving the music track backward or forward six or more frames until, it is hoped, everything suddenly falls into place. It may be that subtle movements or sounds on the screen, which did not feel important enough to log when the timing sheets were written, now seem in conflict with the music. The exact final placement of the music is much like a tightrope walk. Everything has to be taken into account.

There are other options when cutting the music into the film. In an extreme instance, it might be determined that the music written for a certain scene is not needed at all and the cue is then dropped. Considering the effort that went into the composing, this can hurt. Every film composer has sensed at one time or another that when the music is very difficult to come by for a certain section, the reason might be that the music isn't really necessary in the first place. Still, there are borderline cases in which a composer can't be absolutely certain and may decide to write it anyway, knowing that it could be dropped later on. At other times, it may be that the first part of a cue fits well but the second part doesn't. One hopes there is a place to end so that the second part can be omitted. It might be that cuts of this kind would upset the structure and shape of the music, but such cuts are necessary sometimes. If a cut is anticipated a composer might build in a phrase ending someplace, followed by a quarter rest, so that a cut can be made without any apparent disruption to the musical line.

Occasionally, a section of film is found where music seems needed but where none was planned. The dubber will go to the score to find a cue that can be repeated, one that somehow feels right for the new place and that is of the required length. This works sometimes—mostly by accident—but little can be asked of that cue except that it indeed fill in the space.

The print used for the spotting session includes an ambient sound track and dialogue. However, additional sounds and sound effects are ordinarily brought in at the final dubbing. Special effects take longer, and they are put in after the music has been written. At this final point, dialogue, music, sound effects, and ambient sound (background noise) are finally blended into an auditory whole.

Composers are often just as surprised and distracted by the relative loudness of added ambient noises as the others involved with the film are by the added music. It takes a while for everybody to reconcile these new aspects. In the meantime, however, if a certain sound—wind, for example—obliterates the music, the question is: What is more important to the meaning of the scene, the ambient sound or the music? Often, the music is chosen, and the volume of the wind is turned down.

Many composers prefer not to attend the final stages of the dubbing process, feeling their participation would be futile. They naturally wish the music could be louder or that certain ambient sounds could be fewer, especially when they fall at crucial instances in the musical design. The fact that music often becomes obscured in the final edit has prompted the wry observation that composers should invite their friends to the recording session because that is the last time the music will ever be fully heard.

*Aftermath*

At this point, the composer's job is finished—unless, of course, he is called upon to furnish additional music for special reasons. There is one thing yet to look forward to: the screening of the film in a theater with an audience. Whatever misgivings composers might have about their work, and everyone has them, this is an exciting moment. Copland put it well when he said, "It is only in the motion picture theater that the composer for the first time gets the full impact of what he has accomplished, tests the dramatic punch of his favorite musical spot, appreciates the curious importance and unimportance of detail, wishes he had done certain things differently and is surprised that others came off better than he had hoped. For when all is said and done, the art of combining moving pictures with musical tones is still a mysterious art. Not the least mysterious element is the theatergoers' reaction."[25]

# Notes

## Chapter One

1. Leonard Rosenman, lecture at San Francisco State University, fall 1992.
2. David Raksin, lecture at the University of Michigan, Ann Arbor, spring 1978.
3. Sergei Eisenstein, *The Film Sense,* ed. and trans. Jay Leyda (New York: Harcourt, Brace and World, 1949), pp. 163–64.
4. Leonard Rosenman, conversations with the author, 1980.
5. Roy Prendergast, *Film Music: A Neglected Art,* 2d ed. (New York: W. W. Norton, 1992), p. 239.
6. Elmer Bernstein, "The Aesthetics of Film Scoring: A Highly Personal View," *Film Music Notebook* 4, no. 1 (1978).
7. Bernard Herrmann, "Music in Motion Pictures," *New York Times,* 24 June 1945.
8. Ernest Gold, conversations with the author, 1980.
9. Elmer Bernstein, "The Man with the Golden Arm," *Film Music* 15, no. 3 (Spring 1956).
10. John Addison, lecture at the University of Michigan, Ann Arbor, spring 1980.
11. Ibid.

## Chapter Two

1. Gold, conversations.
2. Ibid.
3. Hugo Friedhofer, *Oral History* (Los Angeles: American Film Institute/L. B. Mayer Foundation, Feldman Library, 1974).
4. Addison, lecture.
5. Rosenman, conversations.
6. Leith Stevens, "The Wild One," *Film Music* 13, no. 3 (January–February 1954).

7. Addison, lecture.
8. Ivor Montague, *Film World* (Baltimore: Penguin Books, 1967), p. 155.
9. George Roy Hill, *Film Music Notebook* (Winter 1974).
10. Robert Warshow develops this notion in his book *The Immediate Experience* (New York: Doubleday Anchor, 1964).
11. Gold, conversations.
12. Christopher Palmer, liner notes for *To Kill a Mockingbird,* Warner Bros. Records, 1978.
13. Gold, conversations.
14. Jerry Fielding, conversations with the author, 1978.
15. Siegfried Kracauer, *Theory of Film* (New York: Oxford University Press, 1960), p. 141.
16. Ibid., p. 142.
17. Herman Hupfeld wrote "As Time Goes By" years before the film was made, for a 1931 Broadway musical revue entitled "Everybody's Welcome."
18. Alan S. Downer, "The Film Style of John Huston," *Princeton Quarterly* 29 (Summer 1966): 27–28.
19. Ibid.
20. Ibid.
21. Mark Evans, *Soundtrack: The Music of the Movies* (New York: Hopkinson and Blake, 1975), p. 134.


*Chapter Three*

1. David Raksin, conversations with the author, 1986.
2. Evans, *Soundtrack,* p. 9.
3. Raksin, conversations.
4. Gold, conversations.
5. Ibid.
6. Ibid.
7. Ibid.
8. Leonard Rosenman, conversations with the author, 1990.
9. Raksin, conversations.
10. Gold, conversations.
11. Hall appeared both in the stage production of the play and in the film, which was directed by Altman.
12. Robert Altman, conversations with the author during the making of *Fool for Love,* 1984.
13. Gold, conversations.
14. Rosenman, conversations, 1990.
15. James Goode, *The Story of The Misfits* (Indianapolis and New York: Bobbs-Merrill, 1963), pp. 44–45.
16. Ibid., p. 298.

17. Ibid.
18. Ibid.
19. Ibid., p. 299.
20. Ibid., p. 320.
21. Montague, *Film World,* p. 106.

*Chapter Four*

1. David Raksin, liner notes for *Laura,* RCA ARL1-1490.
2. Ibid.
3. In an interview with Roy Prendergast, in *Film Music,* p. 63.
4. Raksin, conversations.
5. Ibid.
6. Rosenman, conversations, 1980.

*Chapter Five*

1. François Truffaut, *Hitchcock* (New York: Simon & Schuster, 1967), p. 193.
2. Gene Youngblood, *Expanded Cinema* (New York: E. P. Dutton, 1970), p. 105.
3. Rudolph Arnheim, *Film as Art* (Berkeley: University of California Press, 1957), p. 227.
4. Truffaut, *Hitchcock,* p. 234.

*Chapter Six*

1. In an interview with Irwin Bazelon, in Bazelon's *Knowing the Score* (New York: Arco Publishing, 1975), p. 207.
2. Ibid., p. 199.
3. Rosenman, conversations, 1990.
4. Richard Rodney Bennett, interview in *Film Music Notebook* 2, no. 1 (1976).
5. In an interview with Don Wardell for "Music to Commit Murder By," *Soho Weekly News,* 9 September 1976.
6. Altman, conversations.
7. Ibid.
8. Ibid.
9. Gold, conversations.
10. Bruce Knudson, *Project Tempo* (Simi Valley, Calif.: Carroll Knudson, 1965; reprint, Newbury Park, Calif., 1981).
11. Ernest Gold, conversations with the author, 1982.
12. Alex North, conversations with the author, 1984.
13. Leonard Rosenman, conversations with the author, 1985.
14. Rosenman, lecture.
15. Ibid.

16. David Raksin, conversations with the author, 1985.

17. Gold, conversations, 1980.

18. In an interview with Irwin Bazelon, in *Knowing the Score,* pp. 201–2.

19. Ibid., p. 220.

20. Royal S. Brown, "Bernard Herrmann and the Subliminal Pulse of Violence," *High Fidelity* 26 (March 1976): 66.

21. John Addison, conversations with the author, 1980.

22. North, conversations.

23. Gold, conversations, 1980.

24. John Broeck, "Music of the Fears," *Film Comment* 12 (September–October 1976): 57.

25. Aaron Copland, "Tip to Moviegoers: Take Off Those Ear Muffs," *The New York Times Magazine,* 6 November 1949.

# Selected Bibliography

Arnheim, Rudolph. *Film as Art*. Berkeley: University of California Press, 1957.

Bazelon, Irwin. *Knowing the Score*. New York: Arco Publishing, 1975.

Bernstein, Elmer. "The Aesthetics of Film Scoring: A Highly Personal View." *Film Music Notebook* 4, no. 1 (1978).

————. "The Man with the Golden Arm." *Film Music* 15, no. 3 (Spring 1956).

————. "Whatever Happened to Great Film Music?" *High Fidelity and Musical America* 22, no. 7 (July 1972).

Brown, Royal S. "An Interview with Bernard Herrmann." *High Fidelity,* September 1963, pp. 64–67.

Bruce, Graham. *Bernard Herrmann: Film Music and Narrative*. Ann Arbor: UMI Research Press, 1985.

Copland, Aaron. *The New Music*. Rev. ed. (*Our New Music,* 1941). New York: W. W. Norton, 1968.

————. "Tip to Moviegoers: Take Off Those Ear Muffs." *The New York Times Magazine,* 6 November 1949.

Downer, Alan S. "The Film Style of John Huston." *Princeton Quarterly* 29 (Summer 1966).

Eisenstein, Sergei. *The Film Sense*. Edited and translated by Jay Leyda. New York: Harcourt, Brace and World, 1949.

Eisler, Hanns. *Composing for the Films*. New York: Oxford University Press, 1947.

Evans, Mark. *Soundtrack: The Music of the Movies*. New York: Hopkinson and Blake, 1975.

Friedhofer, Hugo. *Oral History*. Los Angeles: American Film Institute/L. B. Mayer Foundation, Feldman Library, 1974.

Gallez, Douglas. "Theories of Film Music." *Cinema Journal* (Spring 1970), pp. 40–47.

Goode, James. *The Story of The Misfits*. Indianapolis and New York: Bobbs-Merrill, 1963.

Gorbman, Claudia. *Unheard Melodies: Narrative Film Music*. Bloomington: Indiana University Press, 1987.

Hagen, Earle. *Scoring for Films*. Rev. ed. Van Nuys, Calif.: Alfred Publishing Co., 1989.

Karlin, Fred, and Wright, Rayburn. *On the Track: A Guide to Contemporary Film Scoring*. New York: Schirmer Books, 1990.

Kracauer, Siegfried. *Theory of Film*. New York: Oxford University Press, 1960.

Limbacher, James L. *Film Music: From Violins to Video*. Metuchen, N.J.: Scarecrow Press, 1974.

———. *Keeping Score: Film Music, 1972–1979*. Metuchen, N.J.: Scarecrow Press, 1981.

London, Kurt. *Film Music: A Summary of the Characteristic Features of Its History, Aesthetics, and Technique; and Its Possible Developments*. Translated by Eric Bensinger. London: Faber and Faber, 1936; reprint, New York: Arno Press, 1970.

Lustig, Milton. *Music Editing for Motion Pictures*. New York: Hastings House Communications Arts Books, 1980.

Manvell, Roger, and Huntley, John. *The Technique of Film Music*. Revised and enlarged by Richard Arnell and Peter Day. New York: Hastings House, 1975.

Mast, Gerald. *A Short History of the Movies*. New York: Bobbs-Merrill, 1971.

Montague, Ivor. *Film World*. Baltimore: Penguin Books, 1967.

Newsom, Jon. *David Raksin: A Composer in Hollywood*. Washington: Library of Congress, 1985.

Palmer, Christopher. *The Composer in Hollywood*. London: Marion Boyars; New York: Rizzoli International, 1990.

———. *Rozza*. London: Criterion Music, 1975.

Prendergast, Roy. *Film Music: A Neglected Art*. 2d ed. New York: W. W. Norton, 1992.

Rhode, Eric. "Hitchcock's Art." *Encounter Magazine*, October 1963.

Rosenman, Leonard. "East of Eden." *Film Music* 14, no. 3 (May–June 1955).

———. "Notes from a Sub-Culture." *Perspectives of New Music* 7, no. 1 (Fall–Winter 1968).

Sharples, Win, Jr. "The Aesthetics of Film Sound." *Filmmakers Newsletter* 8, no. 5 (March 1975), pp. 27–32.

Skinner, Frank. *Underscore*. New York: Criterion Music, 1960.

Steiner, Fred. "Herrmann's Black-and-White Music for Hitchcock's Psycho." *Film Music Notebook* 1, no. 1 (1974), pp. 28–36.

Sternfeld, Frederick W. "Music and Feature Films." *Musical Quarterly* 33, no. 4 (October 1947), pp. 517–32.

Stevens, Leith. "The Wild One." *Film Music* 13, no. 3 ( January–February 1954).

Thomas, Tony. *Music for the Movies*. South Brunswick, N.J., and New York: A. S. Barnes, 1973.

Truffaut, François. *Hitchcock*. New York: Simon & Schuster, 1967.

Warshow, Robert. *The Immediate Experience*. New York: Doubleday Anchor, 1964.

# Glossary of Musical Terms

*allegro*   (It., cheerful) used to indicate a quick or lively tempo.

*arpeggiation*   notes of a chord played one after another rather than simultaneously.

*atonality*   a music compositional approach wherein the notion of a *key* center is suspended. Instead, emphasis is placed on the manipulation of *cells* (or unique combinations of notes) as a means for continuity and development.

*augmentation*   the presentation of a melodic idea in longer durational values, e.g., where quarter-notes become half-notes.

*augmented triad*   a *triad* in which the 5th scale step up from the *root* has been raised a half step (e.g., C-E-G$^\sharp$), usually to intensify motion to a subsequent chord.

*bi-chordal*   a harmony consisting of two different chords played simultaneously.

*cadence*   (from L. cadere, to fall) a melodic or *harmonic progression* that occurs at the end of a composition, a section, or a *phrase,* conveying an impression of a momentary or final conclusion.

*cadential progression*   a succession of chords approaching a structural downbeat or arrival point; occurs at the end of a section or *phrase.*

*canon*   a round (such as "Row, row, row your boat"), wherein one *voice* imitates another.

*cell*   an *interval* or small group of notes used as a basis for development.

*chromatic*   refers to a series of notes a half step apart; also the antithesis of *diatonic.* Chromatic notes therefore are notes not belonging to an established major or minor key.

*cluster*   a collection of adjacent notes played simultaneously (e.g., C-D-D#-E-F).

*coda*   (It., tail) a closing section that absorbs the accumulated energy of what has gone before in order to achieve a sense of finality.

*counterpoint*   where two or more *lines* are set against one another, and each has a sense of independence or integrity of its own. When combined, they make a much larger statement than would be possible by any one of the lines.

*diatonic*   used with reference to a major or minor scale and the notes found therein.

*diminution*   the opposite of *augmentation;* a melodic idea written in reduced time values, e.g., where quarter-notes become eighth-notes.

*dissonance*   a situation wherein a combination of notes within a given musical context (tonal or atonal) produces a sense of instability, creating a need to continue. Dissonance has been explained as a sound that is "harsh," "discordant," or "clashing." The shortcoming of such words lies not so much in the fact that they are based entirely on subjective impressions, but chiefly in their failure to account for changing attitudes toward certain sounds (e.g., the major seventh) as these sounds find new meanings within twentieth-century musical contexts.

*dodecaphonic*   music based on a specific ordering of all twelve notes of the *chromatic* scale as an organizational procedure, i.e., 12-tone or *serial music.*

*dominant*   the fifth degree of the major or minor scale, so called on account of its "dominating" function in tonal harmony as the root of the dominant triad (G-B-D in C major). This triad is most frequently resolved into the tonic triad, called a V-I *harmonic progression.* Because of the falling 5th in this progression (G down to C) the V-I is the strongest *key-*establishing progression in the tonal system.

*downbeat*   the first beat of a measure.

*envelope*   the loudness curve of a note or sound from its onset to its very end.

*episode*   a free section in a *fugue* wherein a *subject entry* is not in progress.

*fifth chords*   chords consisting of perfect fifths stacked one on top of the other.

*fourth chords*   chords consisting of perfect fourths stacked one on top of the other.

*fragment*   a short musical idea consisting of only a few notes; usually taken from a larger melodic idea.

*fugato*   a passage resembling the style and content of a *fugue* exposition (see *fugue*).

*fugue*    a contrapuntal form employing two or more *voices*. In the exposition, each *voice* states the fugue subject (the principal thematic idea) and
a counter subject. The second stage of the fugue consists of additional
*subject entries* and *episodes* in related *keys*. The third stage brings the fugue
back to the *tonic*.

*glissando*    a slide between two notes.

*harmonic function*    the relationship of a chord to the other chords in a *harmonic progression*.

*harmonic progression*    a succession of chords within a given context.

*interval*    the distance between two notes.

*inversion*    the contour of a melodic line played upside down; also a chord
(see *triad*) in which the third, fifth, or seventh appears in the bass.

*key*    a term indicating the *tonality* of a piece in either major or minor.

*legato*    (It., tied) used to indicate that the connection between notes is
played smoothly and without any apparent interruption.

*line*    refers to a single voice or instrumental part.

*Lydian mode*    similar to the major scale but with the fourth degree raised
a half step; the white keys on the piano from F to F.

*meter*    the number of beats in a measure of music; e.g., 3/4 indicates that
there are three quarter-notes or beats in each measure.

*modulation*    the harmonic shift from one key to another within a composition.

*motif, motive*    a distinctive melodic idea within a *theme* that becomes the
basis for further development.

*non-chord pitch*    an individual tone not belonging to the underlying
harmony.

*non-pitch*    any sound that cannot be perceived as a particular note, such as
the sound of a drum.

*orchestration*    the art of writing music for an instrumental ensemble.

*ostinato*    (It., obstinate) a succession of notes or rhythms repeated over and
over again; functions as a structural base for an extended musical passage.

*overture*    an introductory instrumental piece establishing a sense of movement or mood as well as musical material to be used later on.

*pandiatonic*    harmonic style of writing in which all the notes of the *diatonic*
scale are given more or less equal status. Historically, pandiatonicism rep-
resents a reaction against the "pan-chromaticism" of *atonality* as well as
against the "harmonic chromaticism" of the late nineteenth century.

*parallel motion*    two or more musical lines moving in precisely the same
way.

*partials*    the combination of a fundamental pitch and its overtones forming the acoustical content of a given pitch. All musical instruments produce sounds consisting of the fundamental plus a number of additional sounds, called overtones, which are not heard distinctly because their intensity is usually much less than that of the fundamental. The overtones combine to form the richness associated with an instrumental *timbre*.

*pedal point*   a long-held note (most often in the bass) in *counterpoint* to changing harmonies brought about by other *voices*.

*phrase*   a relatively short section of music ending with a *cadence;* musical equivalent to a sentence in grammar.

*pizzicato*   (It., plucked; abbr. *pizz.*) in violin, viola, cello, and bass playing, an indication that the string is to be plucked with the fingers.

*polyphony, polyphonic*   (Gr., polys, *many;* phonos, *voice*) a *texture* involving two or more independent *voices;* practically synonymous with *counterpoint*.

*polytonal (bi-tonal)*   the simultaneous use of two or more *tonal* centers.

*pyramid*   gradual upward addition of pitches resulting in ever-increasing number of *voices* expressed as a chord.

*register*   a particular octave.

*root position harmonies*   *triads* voiced with the name of the chord in the lowest *voice* (e.g., a D chord would have D in the base).

*score*   a representation of instrumental parts; an orchestral page.

*semi-cadence*   a *phrase* ending on the *dominant*

*serial (12-tone) music*   music compositional approach using an ordering of the twelve pitches of the *chromatic* scale as a referential norm; it is a system in which all notes have equal importance, unlike the hierarchical implications in *tonality*.

*sketch*   a short, abbreviated *score,* written on three to nine lines indicating the intended nature of the *orchestration*.

*step progression*   a step-wise descent in the upper *voice* that points up the structural unfolding of the *diatonic* scale in the *key* of the music.

*subject entry*   the principle thematic material as stated by each of the *voices* in a *fugue*.

*suspension*   a note held over from the previous chord creating a *dissonance* with the new harmony.

*tessitura*   given range and characteristics of a particular instrument or voice.

*texture*   1) thickness of orchestration (thus, the more parts doing different things at the same time, the thicker the texture); 2) one of several compositional approaches, including *polyphonic* (contrapuntal), monophonic, homophonic (chordal), and melody and accompaniment.

*theme*   the principal melodic *line* of a piece or section.

*timbre*   the unique sound quality associated with any given musical instrument.

*tonality*   a system whereby the music naturally gravitates to one pitch that is termed the tonal center or *key* of the music.

*tonic*   the first note of the major or minor scale.

*tonic key*   the principal tonal center in a tonal composition.

*tonicize*   to momentarily point up a chord (other than the *tonic*) as a new *tonic* by preceding it with its own *dominant*.

*transition*   a bridge-like passage that consists of a shift from one section to another; usually synonymous with *modulation*.

*triad*   chord of three notes built by thirds (e.g., C-E-G). The notes are referred to as the *root,* the third, and the fifth.

*triad unfoldment*   the notes of a *triad* presented in succession.

*triplet*   a three-note subdivision of a beat.

*tritone*   an *interval* of three whole steps (e.g., F-B); occurs in the major scale between the fourth and seventh scale degrees; an interval that, within a tonal context, demands resolution.

*unison*   more than one *voice* or instrument sounding the same pitch (in the same octave) at the same time.

*upbeat (pick-up)*   the beat just before the *downbeat* of the next measure.

*voice*   generally, a term used for any single *line* of music, whether performed by vocalist or instrumentalist.

*winds*   specifically, woodwind instruments (flutes, oboes, clarinets, bassoons), but often used to include brass instruments.

# Index

*Page numbers in italics indicate musical examples.*

Accent. *See* Musical accent
Acoustic space, 209
Addison, John: *A Bridge Too Far,* 30–31, *31–32;* on the pit orchestra, 14; on role of the orchestrator, 236–37; *Sleuth,* 12, 14, *14–15,* 25, *25–26,* 82; *Tom Jones,* 87; *Torn Curtain,* 215
*Al Capone,* 34–39, *35–38,* 69, 207
Albinoni, Tomaso, 66–67
Altman, Robert, 73, 88, 112, 221–23
Ambient sound, 112, 129, 211–12, 226, 246
*Anderson Tapes, The,* 242
Andrews, Dana, 143–44, 155, 173
Archetypes, 39–41
Arnheim, Rudolph, 213
Association, process of, 9–11
Atmosphere, 11–12
Atonal music, 48–49

Bach, Johann Sebastian, 68
Bacharach, Burt, 33
Baroque style, 25, 66–67, 87
Basie, Count, 70
Basinger, Kim, 112
*Battle of the Bulge, The,* 212

Beat (pulse): coalescence of images, 100–101; inner rhythm, 87; supra rhythmic structure, 88–89; synchronization, 107, 111–12
Benedek, Laszlo, 30
Bennett, Richard Rodney, 218, 221
Bergman, Ingmar, 207
Bernstein, Elmer: *The Man with the Golden Arm,* 11; on music's appeal to the emotions, 10; on recording *Torn Curtain,* 214; *Sweet Smell of Success,* 30; on timings, 228; *To Kill a Mockingbird,* 42–45, *43–44*
*Best Years of Our Lives, The,* 41, *42,* 143–68. *See also* Friedhofer, Hugo
*Between Heaven and Hell,* 9, 64, *65–66,* 88–89, *90–99,* 100
Bichordality, 161–62
*Billy Budd,* 232
*Blazing Saddles,* 70
*Boys from Brazil, The,* 17, 68
Brando, Marlon, 18–19, 21
Brant, Henry, 238
*Bridge Too Far, A,* 30–31, *31–32*
Brooks, Mel, 70
Browne, Richmond, 171

261